CONTENTS

FLOWERS, FLOWERS!

Inspired Arrangements for All Occasions

PAULA PRYKE

PHOTOGRAPHY BY KEVIN SUMMERS

 RIZZOLI
NEW YORK

For my mother and father
who have always been a constant source of inspiration
and love and created beautiful gardens to daydream in.

FLOWERS, FLOWERS!
PAULA PRYKE

Photographs by **KEVIN SUMMERS**

First published in the United States of America in 1993 by
RIZZOLI INTERNATIONAL PUBLICATIONS, INC.
300 Park Avenue South, New York, NY 10010
Reprinted in 1994, 1996
© Mitchell Beazley International Ltd 1993
Text copyright © Paula Pryke 1993

Library of Congress Cataloging-in-Publication Data

Pryke, Paula
     Flowers, flowers! : inspired arrangements for all occasions /
Paula Pryke.
          p.   cm.
     Includes index.
     ISBN 0-8478-1679-6
     1. Flower arrangement. 2. Cut flowers. 3. Flowers. I. Title.
SB449.P79   1993
745.92——dc20   93-862
                                                        CIP

Edited and designed by Mitchell Beazley International Ltd
part of Reed Consumer Books

Art Director **JACQUI SMALL**
Senior Executive Editor **JUDITH MORE**
Art Editor **TRINITY FRY**
Senior Editor **SOPHIE PEARSE**
Production **SARAH SCHUMAN**

The publishers have made every effort to ensure that all instructions given
in this book are accurate and safe, but they cannot accept liability for
any resulting injury, damage or loss to either person or property
whether direct or consequential and howsoever arising. The author
and publishers will be grateful for any information which will
assist them in keeping future editions up to date.

Text filmset in Gill Sans and Bembo by Litho Link, Welshpool, Powys, Wales
Reproduction by Manadarin Offset, Singapore
Produced by Mandarin Offset
Printed and bound in China

The Flower Market

Over the past twenty-five years the cultivation of flowers has become a highly international industry. Today blooms are grown commercially in all corners of the world and increasingly in countries with favourable climates and inexpensive labour. For instance, in parts of Africa and South America and in south-east Asian countries such as Thailand, Malaysia and Singapore, beautiful tropical blooms, in particular Vanda, Dendrobium and Oncidium orchids are grown for the world market. Even as early as 1928 flowers were being transported by air across

before arriving at a destination in Australia and carnations *(Dianthus)* from the Middle East frequently travel via the Netherlands before reaching British flower markets and retail outlets.

It is possible to visit a Dutch flower-producing area or an auction by prior arrangement and this is a fascinating and unforgettable experience which I can highly recommend. For more information contact your Dutch tourist office. Inside the enormous trading complexes you will see a panorama of myriad flowers loaded onto thousands of stacking trolleys which

Gerberas (Gerbera) are some of my favourite cut flowers. The blooms are often grown under glass and are cut daily (left). Each stem is graded according to quality and colour (middle). The flowers are packed into boxes for transportation so that the heads are protected and the stem ends are all cut to an equal length (right).

continents and today quantities of plant material are freighted in this way daily, although within continents and also nationally plant material is usually transported by road. More and more growers worldwide are producing beautiful blooms and foliage in all latitudes and, together with efficient air links and improved methods of packaging and preserving fresh flowers, the international flower market continues to expand on a global scale. Blooms can be picked and packaged on one continent and sold in another within a matter of days, a fact which means that flower enthusiasts the world over can enjoy an increasing number of less familiar varieties.

As far back as the 17th century the Netherlands was establishing itself as the horticultural hub of Europe, and to this day it has retained this position. Today the majority of the world's flowers find their way to one of the enormous Dutch flower auctions. As well as being a major trader and exporter of blooms the Netherlands is an important flower cultivation area. The Dutch grow huge numbers of species under glass all the year around and, in addition, the auctions are supplied with all sorts of plant varieties which do not grow easily in Europe's temperate climate. Some Dutch firms cultivate overseas in order to benefit from different climates and soils, for instance, the beautiful 'Le Reve' lilies *(Lilium ' Le Reve')* which have a delicate pink colouring are cultivated on the West Coast of the United States and pinks *(Dianthus)* and oleanders *(Nerium oleander)* are grown in Portugal. Varieties such as proteas *(Protea)*, agapanthus *(Agapanthus)*, gay feathers *(Liatris)* and cymbidiums *(Cymbidium)* are flown in regularly from African suppliers. A large proportion of the world's blooms are also traded through the Dutch auctions, which act as international flower brokerages. For example, the elegant, long-stemmed French tulips *(Tulipa French)* may pass through the Netherlands en route to Beverly Hills in California, Italian mimosa *(Mimosa)* is often routed through one of the Dutch auctions

are conveyed from cool storage rooms to the trading floor via a complicated network of rails. Employees of the huge auctions often travel through the warehouses in true Dutch fashion – on bicycles!

In the cultivating areas technology is so advanced that in many nurseries plant care is controlled by precisely programmed computer systems so that flowers are automatically watered, fed and harvested, and in some cases music is even played to stimulate growth! Machines are also used to batch flowers into multiples of ten stems and each batch is checked by hawk-eyed quality controllers for any sign of pests or disease. The batches are then strictly graded according to colouring, general condition and the length of the stems: the longer the stems the more valuable the batch. After careful grading the blooms are automatically wrapped in order to prevent the flower heads from bruising during transit. For instance, gerberas *(Gerbera)* are packaged in special boxes so that the heads are supported above a flat surface and the stems are inserted through a small hole and hang underneath. Very delicate varieties, such as some types of orchids and also painter's palettes *(Anthurium)* and amaryllis *(Hippeastrum)*, are often individually wrapped so that the petals are protected and other fragile stems may have a tube filled with a solution of plant feed attached to the stem end, in order to prevent wilting. Potted varieties are carefully wedged into trays and bunches of blooms, which are sold in batches of ten stems, are wrapped in paper or cellophane to prevent damage.

Every effort is made to ensure that the flowers remain in good condition throughout the chain of grower to auction to wholesaler to retailer, until finally reaching the customer. Exporters, wholesalers and also shopkeepers and street vendors attend the international auctions and acquire flowers by bidding not under a hammer, but against one of several large electronic clocks which are a feature of the Dutch auctions. Instead of the bidding

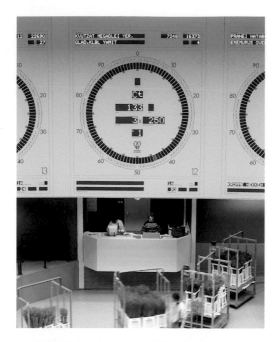

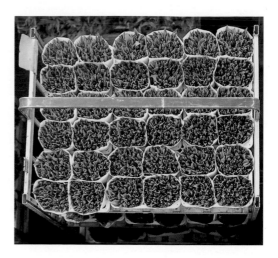

Left: Flowers sold at the international Dutch auctions come not under a hammer but under an electronic clock.
Above: Within the auction complex all fresh stems are transported in water-filled crates stacked onto trolleys.

Above: An overhead view of crates of cut tulip (Tulipa) stems loaded onto a trolley before they are transported to the auction hall in order to be sold. The flowers are all graded according to colour, condition and length of stem.

Above: Blooms are protected by a paper wrapping in order to maintain their peak condition and their value.
Below: Many types of foliage, including ornamental twigs are sold at auction. Here two varieties of willow (Salix) are grouped into bundles of equal quantities for auctioning.

Above: The delicate heads of grape hyacinths (Muscari) are protected by cellophane prior to entering the auction.
Below: All sorts of tropical leaves are available at auction, as they provide valuable decorative florist's material. Here 'Chico' leaves are tied and wrapped in equal numbers.

Above: Daffodils (Narcissus) are sold while still in bud and are boxed for transportation. One open flower is raised to show buyers what the blooms will look like once open.
Below: Bundles of galax (Galax) leaves grown in Florida are wrapped in damp newspaper to increase longevity.

Below left: These 'Jacaranda' roses (Rosa 'Jacaranda') are in poor condition and are an example of what not to purchase when you are buying flowers. You should avoid flowers with faded petals and pale stems and leaves. Weak colouring, and also the small heads of these roses, indicate that they were probably grown out of season and under artificial glass-house conditions. Even though some European cultivators install all-night lights in order to simulate natural sunlight, flowers grown out of doors in countries with favourable climates (for example Israel and Columbia) are of better quality. Roses which look like these may also have spent too much time stored in a chill room and may not open fully once arranged indoors.
Below right: These 'Jaguar' roses (Rosa 'Jaguar') are in good condition. Roses worth buying should have strong stems and closed sepals. The petals and also the stems and foliage should have strong colouring. Gently feel the heads of roses before making a purchase: they should be firm and not soft, otherwise they may not open.

Above and right: All stems are graded according to length. The longer the stems of 'First Red' roses (Rosa 'First Red') or plum (Prunus) blossom, the greater their value.

starting low and gradually building up as is the case in some auctions, the clock first displays a maximum opening price for each lot of flowers. This price then begins to drop on the digital clock face until, at the press of a button, the first bidder interrupts the descending price scale – the lot is then sold for the price indicated on the clock. At certain times of the year particular varieties are in great demand and so keep the bidding at an unusually high level. For example, prior to Saint Valentine's Day on 14 February red roses _(Rosa)_ are at a premium, longi lilies _(Lilium longiflorum)_ are especially popular for national religious festivals and Saints' Days, while during the wedding season, which coincides with mid-summer months in northern climes, popular bridal flowers such as stephanotis _(Stephanotis)_ increase dramatically in price at auction and consequently in retail outlets.

Europe is an important growing area and also a significant consumer in the world flower market. For example, Germany produces very high-quality roses _(Rosa)_, France grows excellent orchids, lilac _(Syringa)_ and ranunculus _(Ranunculus)_. The French also export the largest and most exquisite snapdragons _(Antirrhinum)_ and stocks _(Matthiola)_. In Italy the main growing areas are along the Riviera, although because cultivation is usually out of doors sadly entire crops are sometimes lost to late frosts. My favourite Italian exports are forget-me-nots _(Myosotis)_, eucalyptus pods _(Eucalyptus)_, butcher's broom _(Ruscus)_ and anemones _(Anemone)_. In Scandanavian countries, and also in Belgium and Switzerland, potted plants are particularly popular and consequently these are exported in greater quantities than cut flowers. In Britain the flower-growing industry is still relatively unmechanized and only chrysanthemums _(Chrysanthemum)_ are produced on a large scale. Domestically, seasonal

daffodils _(Narcissus)_ and tulips _(Tulipa)_ are abundant and British growers also cultivate lovely arum lilies _(Zantedeschia)_ and excellent sweet peas _(Lathyrus odoratus)_. Although all sorts of flowers can be grown successfully indoors and all the year around under the controlled conditions of a glass-house environment, it is very difficult to propagate sweet peas out of their natural growing season. Nor are these delightful blooms simple to transport – crowded together they tend to overheat and suffocate each other and so wilt easily. The most robust sweet peas are those that are homegrown in the garden, but even these are rarely hardy or long-lasting. The Channel Islands are known for their wonderful freesia _(Freesia)_ and smilax _(Asparagus asparagoides)_ which are exported worldwide.

Flower lovers in North America are supplied with all sorts of home-grown varieties, many of which are cultivated along the West Coast. Plenty of blooms are also supplied by Central and South American countries, in particular Columbia, Mexico and Ecuador, and, as with everywhere else in the world, a large proportion of flowers imported to the United States come from the Netherlands. Conversely, blooms such as birds of paradise _(Strelitzia reginae)_, which grow almost like weeds in California, are prized in Europe for their beauty, and foliage such as bear grass _(Dasylirion)_, galax _(Galax)_ leaves and leatherleaf _(Chamaedaphne calyculata)_ are also exported from various American states to keen buyers in Europe.

In the Netherlands, and also in Japan and North America, extensive glass-house cultivation means that flowers are grown in artificial conditions all the year around. The creation of indoor growing environments where soil, temperature, humidity and plant nutrition are all carefully monitored has broken many of the old limitations of natural growing seasons. A good example of this phenomenon is the tulip _(Tulipa)_. This symbol of the Netherlands is cultivated there thoughout the year and, even when supplies run short during the coldest months of the year supplementary stems are imported from Australia and New Zealand in order to answer huge domestic and international demand. Anemones _(Anemone)_ and peonies _(Paeonia)_ are also imported from Australasia to provide welcome blooms and colour during the winter in northern climes when fresh flowers are less abundant than during the spring and summer periods. Australia and New Zealand also produce flowers such as banksia _(Banksia)_ which has a decorative wiry orange flower head, and appropriately named kangaroo paw _(Anigozanthos)_, which has tubular, slightly furry small flowers.

It is important to always take a careful look at cut flowers before making a purchase, whether you buy them from a flower shop, an open-air stall or

*From top to bottom:
Hawiian painter's palettes
(Anthurium) are carefully
wrapped in order to keep
them warm and also to
prevent people touching
them; as sweat can ruin
the face of the flower.
The heads of 'French'
tulips (Tulipa 'French'),
grown near Nice, on the
Côte d'Azur, are protected
by plastic wire netting.
Soft, bright green bun
moss grown in the moist,
cool climate of Wales
is sold in small boxes.
A large trolley at New
Covent Garden in London,
the largest wholesale flower
market in Britain, loaded
with a morning's shopping.
Flowers on sale at a stall
in New Covent Garden.*

a wholesale source, in order to determine their condition. Blooms which have been cultivated out of doors benefit greatly from natural sunlight and consequently have healthy dark-green stems and leaves. Conversely, flowers grown out of their natural season under artificial conditions often have weaker stems and paler petals and foliage and they will probably not last as well as varieties grown as Nature intended.

The best source of flowers for most arrangers is a well-stocked florist. As a customer it pays to establish a friendly relationship with a retailer whose stock and style of arranging you like. The florist will then not only learn your particular tastes, but will give you advice on how to present flowers so that they look their best and last their longest, and she or he will also be ready to order you special varieties which may otherwise be difficult to obtain. Although some outdoor flower stalls supply perfectly healthy flowers, on the whole cut blooms do not benefit from standing outside for long periods, particularly if it is windy or drafty. Because more and more commercially grown flowers now travel long distances between the grower, auction and wholesale market before finally reaching a retail outlet and becoming available to you as a customer, it is something of a rarity today to find an absolutely fresh shop-bought flower. Before they reach the customer most stems have been in transit and stored in cool rooms for several days. However, if you buy plant material from a regular supplier then she or he should sell you blooms and foliage in a healthy condition which have plenty of life left in them. You should never be afraid to ask your florist questions on how to care for flowers, what special treatment may be necessary and how long they should last. Florists should be happy to advise you and share their experience and expertise.

Every good florist follows the general principles of flower arranging to a certain extent, although some may adapt and develop their own methods. The advice I give in the Techniques section at the back of this book should be taken as guidelines rather than as strict rules, and applying these methods should help you to overcome practical problems and gain the necessary know-how to create more ambitious arrangements. With flower arrangements of any theme subjective taste naturally plays an important part, but certain aspects of design are fundamental to successful results, namely the shape, proportion, balance and harmony of the overall effect.

Everyone enjoys flowers and people often ask me how they can increase the longevity of plant material, as nobody likes to see blooms wilt and die. This is especially frustrating if you have just bought some beautiful stems which then refuse to open or shrivel and turn brown almost as soon as you have taken them home. The truth behind all the myths concerning the preservation of cut flowers – advice ranges from adding aspirin, sugar, lemonade, chlorine or even vodka or a copper coin to water in a container – is that all cut stems do benefit from water enriched with a small dose of sugar. A small amount of anti-bacterial agent such as ordinary household bleach will also keep the water in the container clean and germ-free which helps to increase longevity of the stems. Although a teaspoon of sugar and a drop of bleach dissolved in water in a container will work almost as effectively as a commercial cut-flower feed, it may be easier to use the latter as the manufacturer will give you precise mixing instructions.

It is impossible to generalize about what precisely a buyer should look for when purchasing flowers, as each variety has individual traits. However, in the main you should buy flowers in bud and then condition them by placing them in clean water for several hours before arranging. If the flowers have been deprived of water previous to your purchase then the stems will have begun to dry out and so water absorption is difficult – this is the most common cause of flowers dying prematurely and is often the reason behind disappointingly short-lived roses (Rosa). All cut stems absorb water, and if the water you place them in for conditioning is not

Above and left: This Dutch wholesale flower van is a familiar sight in European cities. The van is especially cooled to keep the cut flowers fresh during their travels. Both sides of the van roll up to reveal trays of beautiful blooms which can be purchased by flower traders. Within Europe plant material is generally transported by road in order to supply shops all over the continent.

clean then they will also absorb dirt and germs which then clog up the vessels in the stem and consequently obstruct further water absorption, so reducing longevity. It is best to give flowers lukewarm (instead of very cold) water to drink and it is important not to forget to cut the ends of stems before arranging them as this facilitates drinking.

This book is arranged into various sections. First, I introduce a thematic approach to flower arranging, giving ideas for selecting and displaying all sorts of plant material according to period and modern, formal and informal, tropical, scented and edible themes. Then I focus on the importance of containers, which are an integral part of the overall floral composition. The right container will complement and highlight the flowers and foliage and in so doing will create an impression of pleasing harmony to the eye and, conversely, making the wrong choice can ruin the whole effect. There are all sorts of suggestions for using glass, pottery, wood, wicker, metal and also a host of imaginative "natural" containers adapted from plant material, including foliage, fruits and vegetables. The next section concentrates on colour themes and takes a close look at the different moods created by red, yellow, green, blue, white and also mixed blooms. Although the question of colour and chromatic combinations is a

highly subjective one, there are certain useful guidelines to follow. The final section of the book covers flower arranging for all sorts of special occasions, from annual festivals such as the New Year, Easter, Halloween, Thanksgiving and Christmas to important personal events such as weddings and anniversaries, birthdays, Mother's Day and Saint Valentine's Day and also giving flowers to friends and loved ones whether in celebration or in sympathy. In all, there are dozens of ideas for creating special arrangements using a rich and exciting variety of flowers and foliage, from the simplest small-scale posy to the grandest one-off display. You should refer to the Techniques section at the back of the book for practical help.

Flower arranging, even for hard-working, professional florists, should be a pleasure; the beauty and huge variety of plant materials available today are a source of constant inspiration to the arranger and a delight to the beholder. There is an old saying in the Netherlands which reflects the Dutch appreciation of flowers and sums up my feelings exactly: "If you have but two guilder in your pocket, buy a loaf of bread with one, and with the other buy a hyacinth for your soul." There is no denying that flowers have an uplifting effect on us all and that they have a place anywhere and everywhere in our lives.

Below: Although many flower vendors display their wares outside, blooms do not benefit from cold drafts.

Below: Inside my flower shop the blooms are arranged on different levels so that customers see the array clearly.

Below: Good florists will sell ready-made bunches of colour-coordinated blooms; these make ideal gifts.

Selecting
a Theme

Whatever your level of skill in flower arranging, the single most important rule is that you should choose blooms and foliage which *you* like and try to arrange them in order to emphasize their natural grace. Over-arranging is a common pitfall and tends to make flowers look stiff and static. Whatever theme you decide to work to – Period, Modern, Simple, Formal, Informal, Tropical, Scented or Edible – instinct and subjectivity should play a part.

When choosing a theme there are various factors you should consider. What is the setting for your flowers? What purpose are the flowers to fulfil – are they for a special occasion, a party or a gift? What budget are you working to? What colour schemes or particular likes and dislikes should you take into account if you are giving flowers away? What special seasonal varieties may be available that you should make the most of in order to keep the cost down? How long should your arrangement last and what is the longevity of the flowers? Whatever the occasion flowers make a statement, indeed they are so expressive of mood that even the smallest sprigs in a tiny vase will not go unnoticed.

There are two main principles behind arranging flowers: a linear design and a massed shape. Within these two different approaches come all sorts of other styles. The linear arrangement is traditional to the East and its tenets can be followed for both simple and modern themes. The Japanese art of flower arranging, "ikebana", began to influence florists in the West at the beginning of the 20th century. All ikebana, and pseudo-ikebana, is characterized by restraint and one advantage to this is that it allows you to create modern themes at times of the year when flowers are in short supply: bare branches are an important component for Japanese arrangers and are well suited to modern displays.

The extraordinary number of refined, minimalist design variations which ikebana specialists create from a limited amount of material should be an inspiration when arranging simple and modern themes. The Oriental emphasis on using seasonal and readily available material is another approach you can take – it also makes sound economic sense! Although ikebana may appear simple, it is by no means free from artifice. For instance, branches should never lean on the rim of a container and because angles and lines are all-important, mechanics such as florist's foam, chicken wire, pin holders and wiring are relied upon to simulate natural growth.

The massed style is documented throughout the long history of Western art. The period theme arrangement on page 21 illustrates this approach perfectly, giving an overall impression of profusion and density of plant material. This display is in fact made up of a mass of individual lines as the stems radiate out from the container. To give a massed arrangement some variation in texture and colour, you should place large flower heads in the middle of the mass in order to draw the eye and provide a focus, and fill in any gaps with foliage to ensure that the display has an even density throughout. Prints and paintings of flower arrangements will offer plenty of inspiration for creating period themes, in particular the lavish still-life canvases of the 16th- and 17th-century Dutch and Flemish artists. These pictures depict the colourful exuberance and fine botanical detail of all sorts of fashionable flowers of the times, for instance the full-blown heads of narcissi *(Narcissus)*, delphiniums *(Delphinium)*, all kinds of lilies *(Lilium)* and roses *(Rosa)*, aquilegias *(Aquilegia)*, irises *(Iris)*, anemones *(Anemone)*, carnations *(Dianthus)* and most typically, tulips *(Tulipa)*.

You can recreate authentic details of a period still life by using blooms which are not naturally in season with each other (this is not difficult nowadays as international flower markets produce flowers in glass-house conditions all the year around) and by placing a few pieces of fruit at the foot of the container. Broken stems and bold combinations of colours and types of flower are all part of this *théâtre végétal* style.

There are currently over 3,000 varieties of tulip in existence, a fact which illustrates their global popularity. This flower which is so characteristic of the period 17th-century genre is equally suitable as part of a simple theme. There is little less fussy and more attractive than a bunch of tulips in a glass fishbowl. The simple one-colour display of crown imperials *(Fritillaria imperialis)* on pages 28-9 gains impact because the flowers are not mixed with any other varieties. To create a simple theme you can either make a bunch of just one type of flower, or limit the display to a maximum of two or three varieties. Or you can restrict the number of colours, selecting perhaps a yellow display of freesias *(Freesia)*, Peruvian lilies *(Alstroemeria ligtu)* and snowberries *(Symphoricarpos albus)*; or a two-colour combination of either blue cornflowers *(Centaurea cyanus)* and creamy ranunculus *(Ranunculus)* or red valerian *(Centranthus ruber)* and white lilac *(Syringa)*. Another way to create a simple arrangement is to keep it small and use tea cups and little vases filled with short-stemmed, delicate flowers which would otherwise be swamped in a larger display. For instance, place a small jugful of buttercups *(Ranunculus)*, gentians *(Gentiana)*, primroses *(Primula vulgaris)*, grape hyacinths *(Muscari)*, pansies *(Viola)*, columbine *(Aquilegia)*, masterwort *(Astrantia)* or marigolds *(Calendula)* on a window ledge or shelf where other larger containers may not fit.

Modern and simple themes share the advantage of being relatively quick, easy and inexpensive to execute. As with simple arrangements you will not need a huge amount of plant material to make a modern arrangement, and you should avoid the temptation of using too many stems. The aim is to achieve a minimalist effect by leaving space and air around the flowers in order to give them maximum impact. There are several points to bear in mind when selecting a modern theme. First, will this style suit the interior it is to be designed for? An abstract arrangement will be in keeping with a plain-coloured room with little clutter and contemporary furnishings, but will look out of place in a room with ornate, patterned or period decoration. You should always set a modern display against a plain background and use an unfussy container which will complement your chosen flowers. Second, because modern themes involve fewer stems, whatever you select should be striking in terms of colour and form. You should try and achieve a contrast of shape and texture with your plant material - for instance, note how the sinuous hardness of the tortured willow *(Salix matsudana 'Tortuosa')* juxtaposes the scarlet heliconias *(Heliconia)* on pages 24-5. You should mix the spiky with the smooth, the vivid with the matte and the velvety with the bobbled. Flowers with unusual forms are always interesting to look at and will create an impression, for example the large heads of proteas *(Protea)* which look almost like an artichoke, the knobbly heads of fernleaf yarrow *(Achillea filipendulina)*, the wirey godetia *(Clarkia)*, the conical pitcher plant *(Sarracenia)*, the waratah *(Telopea)* and the crinkled yellows, reds and pinks of celosia *(Celosia argentea)*. For a modern composition see the right-hand display on page 17. Here a block of wet florist's foam covered with sedum *(Sedum)* provides a base for a phalaenopsis orchid *(Phalaenopsis)*, gloriosas *(Gloriosa superba 'Rothschildiana')*, snake grass *(Scirpus tabernaemontani 'Zebrinus')* and a pitcher plant *(Sarracenia)*.

For special occasions formal themes are most appropriate and usually require more expensive showy flowers and lush foliage to create a striking impact. The first hurdle of formal arranging is to think big, as the overall effect will probably be seen from a distance. In the classical display on pages 32-3 the arrangement was at least 6.5ft (2m) tall. It is important to choose a suitably formal container to set off your flowers, although a bucket will suffice as long as it is disguised with moss, foliage or straw. You can make any modern stoneware pot or urn look antique by staining it with shades of gray, brown, yellow or green emulsion (latex paint), using a rag or flicking the paint onto the stone surface with an old toothbrush. As well as working with long stems so that your arrangement has height, I suggest that you limit the number of different colours and varieties you include to maintain a note of formality. If there is too much of a medley of plant material the display will begin to look messy. You should choose bold flowers with large heads which will be noticed, as small blooms will only get lost. Formal themes include swags and garlands of foliage which can be draped over banisters, chimneypieces and doorways, as well as bouquets, candelabra arrangements and balls of flowers hung from the ceiling for a party; all these are covered in the Special Occasions chapter, see pages 118-69. Because most formal arrangements are sizeable, you will need to employ mechanics such as florist's foam, chicken wire, garden canes and cones or tubes to give stems extra length. All these tools of the trade are explained in the Techniques section at the back of the book.

In the past, the rose *(Rosa)*, the lily *(Lilium)* and the iris *(Iris)* have been adopted as emblems of royalty and nobility and seem to have retained their formal image. You can make an instant grand gesture with a serene bunch of half-opened roses, a few stems of exquisite orchids or some lily heads in a porcelain or glass vase. Lilies in the northern hemisphere are relatively expensive flowers to buy, but they last well and you don't need an excessive number to create an effect. All sorts of attractive varieties are available, including the bold orange 'Enchantment' lily *(Lilium 'Enchantment')*, the yellow 'Limelight' lily *(Lilium 'Limelight')*, the white 'Bright Star' lily *(Lilium 'Bright Star')*, the spotted golden-rayed lily *(Lilium auratum)*, the pink speciosum lily *(Lilium speciosum rubrum)*, and the frilly nerine lily *(Nerine)*. Irises and gladioli *(Gladiolus)*, or sword lilies as they are also called, are other formal, long-stemmed flowers which are worth considering for formal themes. There are small varieties of both types and they have been bred to come in all sorts of shades. The gladiolus in particular is available in almost every colour except blue.

Different precepts apply when arranging flowers informally. You can use all sorts of plant material which you have gathered from friendly neighbours or picked from your garden – and these may be much better than commercially grown flowers. A large bunch of snowdrops *(Galanthus)*, old-fashioned daffodils *(Narcissus)* or sprigs of forsythia *(Forsythia)*, mimosa *(Acacia)* and catkins make an attractive array of flowers placed in a pitcher. As with any theme, it is important to choose a suitable container to match the flowers, and informal arrangements look best in plain wooden trugs, wicker baskets or earthenware and terra-cotta pots. You can group all sorts of plants and flowering bulbs such as cyclamen *(Cyclamen)*, hyacinths *(Hyacinthus)*, heather *(Calluna vulgaris)*, polyanthus *(Primula)*, cowslips *(Primula veris)* and narcissi *(Narcissus)* in a basket lined with plastic to make it waterproof and infilled with bun moss. There are no strictures to arranging informally – you should follow your instinct and feel free to mix colours and varieties spontaneously, and if the overall result has an impromptu feel then so much the better! All sorts of flowering herbs mix well with cut flowers, including dill *(Anethum graveolens)*, fennel *(Foeniculum vulgare)*, lavender *(Lavandula)*, Lady's mantle *(Alchemilla mollis)*, wormwood *(Artemisia)*, 'Jackman's Blue' rue *(Ruta graveolens 'Jackman's Blue')* and hops *(Humulus lupulus)*. There is plenty of room for untamed foliage which breaks any rigidity in the arrangement – twigs of larch *(Larix)*, hornbeam *(Carpinus betulus)*, pussy willow *(Salix caprea)*, wood spurge *(Euphorbia amygdaloides)*, and the hanging velvety tassels of love-lies-bleeding *(Amaranthus caudatus)* all give flow and movement. Or you can loosely arrange long stems of spiraea *(Spiraea)*, all sorts of fruit blossoms, cow parsley *(Anthriscus sylvestris)*, whitebeam *(Sorbus aria)*, onion heads *(Allium)*, foxgloves *(Digitalis)* and love-in-a-mist *(Nigella damascena)* in a tall vase. The beauty of informal themes is that they are quick and easy to put together and no wiring is needed (in fact, wires are out of bounds as they tend to make the stems look artificial). For an informal composition, see the snowberries *(Symphoricarpos albus)*, gomphrena *(Gomphrena)* and white trachelium *(Trachelium)* on the left of page 16.

When choosing flowers for a tropical theme you should aim primarily to create an arrangement full of colour and vibrancy, and you can include tropical fruits to complete the effect. Pineapples *(Ananas comosus)*, pomegranates *(Punica granatum)*, the oriental tomato-like kaki *(Diopyros kaki)*, Chinese dates or jujubes *(Zizyphus jujuba)*, kumquats *(Fortunella)*, which look like miniature oranges, Barbados gooseberries *(Pereskia aculeata)*, which are the edible fruit of a cactus, guavas *(Psidium guajava)*, lychees *(Litchi chinensis)*, mangos *(Mangifera)*, passion fruit *(Passiflora)* and Malaysian rambutans *(Nephelium lappaceum)* are all colourful and decorative varieties which can be wired into an arrangement. Two of my favourite tropical flowers are painter's palettes *(Anthurium)* and birds of paradise *(Strelitzia)* which can be mixed with fronds of date palm *(Phoenix dactylifera)* and fan palm *(Trachycarpus)* for a colourful effect. If you want to create a large tropical arrangement for a party, you can add potted plants with spiky leaves and vibrant flowers – for example, varieties of guzmanias *(Guzmania)*, vriseas *(Vrisea)* and neoregelias *(Neoregelia)*. See the right-hand arrangement on page 16 for a tropical-style composition of king proteas *(Protea cynaroides)* and papyrus grass *(Cyperus papyrus)*.

Scented themes offer all sorts of possibilities from the heady varieties of "old" roses and all sorts of heavenly-scented lilies to delicate sweet peas *(Lathyrus odoratus)*, freesias *(Freesia)*, lily-of-the-valley *(Convallaria majalis)*, stocks *(Matthiola)*, pinks *(Dianthus)*, lilac *(Syringa)*, wax flowers *(Stephanotis floribunda)* and violets *(Viola odorata)*, not to mention a host of aromatic herbs. It is best not to mix heavily-scented flowers in the same arrangement as their smells will clash. Instead, arrange a bunch of potent blooms together or intermixed with unscented varieties. A fragrant arrangement will attract not only the eye but the nose and because of its sweet-smelling quality it will have all the more appeal.

The Renaissance and Dutch masters painted tables piled high with sumptuous fruits and vegetables. Edible themes are ideal to add a special touch to the middle of a table for a dinner party or a celebration meal. There are endless varieties of fruits to make use of: cherries *(Prunus avium)*, quinces *(Cydonia oblonga)*, strawberries *(Fragaria)*, bunches of grapes *(Vitis vinifera)*, rhubarb *(Rheum rhaponticum)*, Chinese lanterns *(Physalis)*, prickly pears *(Opuntia ficusindica)* and star fruits *(Averrhoa carambola)*. As well as fruit you can use all sorts of nuts – chestnuts *(Castanea sativa)*, hazel nuts *(Corylus)*, almonds *(Prunus amygdalus)*, pecans *(Carya illinoiensis)* – and berries – blackberries *(Rubus fruiticosus)*, gooseberries *(Ribes reticulata)*, red currants *(Ribes rubrum)* and mulberries *(Morus rubra, nigra)*. Today vegetables are regarded as more than culinary ingredients and are finding their way into flower shops – for example, bouquets of red and white ornamental cabbages *(Brassica oleracea capitata alba)* are sold as indoor plants. You can construct edible wreaths from vegetables to liven up a kitchen or to give as a gift to an enthusiastic cook. To do this make a wreath base from straw, vine or moss (see page 132) and wire in all sorts of vegetables, particularly the small varieties, such as globe artichokes *(Cynara scolymus)*, asparagus *(Asparagus officinalis)*, miniature sweet corn *(Zea mays)*, sweet peppers *(Capsicum)* and hot "chili" peppers *(Capsicum frutescens)*, garlic bulbs *(Allium sativum)*, baby courgettes *(Cucurbita pepo)*, radishes *(Raphanus sativus)*. Fresh herbs such as parsley *(Petroselinum crispum)* and chives *Allium schoenoprasum)* are also decorative (see page 17). It is important to wire edible arrangements securely as the materials are heavy and to prevent the display becoming too weighty in appearance infill any gaps with aromatic herbs, pine cones and nuts.

PERIOD THEMES

Flowers have been an essential part of our lives and cultures since time began. Artefacts remain from the earliest civilizations which show us the importance and significance that flowers held for our ancestors. Archaeological finds, engravings, paintings, tapestries, architectural motifs, and designs on carpets, porcelain and fabrics all catalogue the history of flowers and their eminence in times gone by.

Since the Bronze Age the Greeks showed their reverence toward flowers in architecture, art, literature and mythology and many pottery and ceramic remains are decorated with grasses, crocuses *(Crocus)*, lilies *(Lilium)*, myrtle *(Myrtus)* and grape vines *(Vitis vinifera)*. While the Greeks were great lovers of flowers in their natural forms, the Romans were formal gardeners and landscapers. They garlanded arches, pillars and doorways with swags of blossom and foliage. Topiary was ubiquitous, plants were sculpted like stonework and ivies and fruit trees were neatly trained. Flowers were gathered in baskets and carried by the Romans in flower-filled scarves held across the body rather like an apron. Garland makers were the florists of the times and wealthy households employed garlanders alongside their gardeners to produce garlands all the year around. Emperors wore chaplets of leaves tied with ribbons at the back of the neck, while strewing flowers and petals at festivals and processions or over guests at meals was another typical custom. The *thyrsus*, a tall, slim staff carried during the festivals of Dionysus and Bacchus was twined with trails of ivy *(Hedera)* as an antidote for drunkenness!

During the Byzantine Empire the Persians and Turks were also noted for their love of flowers and for formal, highly stylized arrangements. Shallow bowls, baskets, ewers and jugs appear in their mosaics, filled with myrtle *(Myrtus)*, acanthus *(Acanthus)*, rosemary *(Rosmarinus officinalis)*, anemones *(Anemone)*, roses *(Rosa)* and lilies *(Lilium)*. The Byzantine fondness for tall, tapering cones decorated with foliage, flowers and fruits in all sorts of colours has left a legacy to modern floral design.

In Medieval times in Europe there was a rather more utilitarian attitude to flowers. They were used in the preparation of food and drink, as medicines, for decorations and for their scent. They played a part in religious symbolism, and Medieval monasteries cultivated herbs and flowers in large "infirmary gardens". Bluebells *(Hyacinthoides)* were cultivated for the starch found in their bulbs, marigolds *(Calendula)* were used to colour cheese and curdle milk, woodruff *(Galium odoratum)* was used to stuff mattresses, and the dye from broom *(Genista)*, when mixed with the blue dye of the woad plant *(Isatis tinctoria)*, produced a much sought-after green colour.

From the time of the Renaissance Europe flowered intellectually and artistically and there was a golden age of horticulture. As trade routes opened up, new species were imported and exported, gardeners became more skilful, and irrigation, grafting and propagating improved. Lavender *(Lavandula)*, roses *(Rosa)* and carnations *(Dianthus)* seem to have been the most favoured flowers of the time. During the 16th century flowers were prized not only for their scent but also for their shape and detail. A taste for decorative flowers such as the crown imperial *(Fritillaria imperialis)*, reflected the fashion for rich, brocaded and intricately embroidered clothes. Double primroses *(Primula)*, daffodils *(Narcissus)* and peonies *(Paeonia)* were grown in all sorts of varieties for their elaborate shapes, although many of these have since disappeared.

At the end of the 16th century the Dutch flower artist Jan Bruegel was one of the first painters to portray detailed, face-on flower arrangements set against dark backgrounds. The 17th-century Flemish and Dutch schools often depicted hybrid flowers such as the striped and feathered varieties of tulips *(Tulipa)* which were so sought-after. Meanwhile, on the other side of the Atlantic in colonial North America, European immigrants were adapting their plants and seeds to a new country and climate. At the same time, dried plants began to be used for decorative rather than simply culinary and medicinal purposes. The flowers included helichrysum *(Helichrysum)*, globe thistle *(Echinops ritro)* and honesty *(Lunaria)*.

The ever-popular rose *(Rosa)* was a very common decorative motif of the 18th century. With the rise of Rococo interior decoration, free, curving lines, ribbons, strong pastel shades and a degree of frivolity influenced contemporary flower arranging. Flowers began to be part of everyday dress and were worn by women as hair, shoe and neckline accessories, a fashion which continued well into the 19th century. There then came an explosion of botanical activity as more and more new plants were discovered by plant-hunting expeditions throughout the 19th century. Rhododendrons *(Rhododendron)*, primulas *(Primula)*, lilies *(Lilium)*, gentians *(Gentiana)* and the famous blue poppy *(Papaver)* were all brought back from remote regions of the world. During the 19th century there were great collectors, hybridizers and cultivators of flowers and it is during this period that the craft of flower arranging developed a pace. For women confined to the home, flower arranging became a domestic and social accomplishment and hostesses of grand balls created floral pavements like mosaic floors, giant indoor rockeries and entire walls of flowers.

The most enduring legacy of 19th-century flower arranging is the posy. Most commonly wired into concentric circles, they were carried by women on all sorts of occasions. Most posies were encircled with a frill of lace or foliage and the middle flower would normally be a rose. Enamel, porcelain and silver "posy holders" would hold the posy upright while ladies paid each other social visits. The brash and bold colours of geraniums *(Pelargonium)*, begonias *(Begonia)* and dahlias *(Dahlia)* were also popular at this time. Greenhouses were heated by complicated systems of coal-fuelled pipes so that stephanotis *(Stephanotis)*, mock orange *(Philadelphus coronarius)*, gardenias *(Gardenia)*, camellias *(Camellia)*, cyclamen *(Cyclamen)* and azaleas *(Azalea)* could be grown.

Flowers were integral to the inspiration behind the Art Nouveau movement, and lilies *(Lilium)*, poppies *(Papaver)*, acanthus *(Acanthus)*, roses *(Rosa)* and tulips *(Tulipa)*, often entwined with ivy *(Hedera)*, were common motifs. Art Nouveau caused Europeans to re-evaluate the concept of beauty in plant terms, and for the first time the scope of floral appreciation was extended to buds, stems and tendrils, and foliage could stand alone. The organic lines of Art Nouveau were a striking contrast to the traditionally symmetrical and often triangular-shaped arrangements of the time which gave a stiffness and formality to flower displays. This conventional and rather rigid style is still the florist's standard today, although the 20th century has seen all sorts of innovations and interpretations, influenced by trends in design and art. These changes were apparent from the beginning of the 20th century onward, when the use of simple seedhead arrangements and Charles Rennie Mackintosh's bowlfuls of coloured twigs pre-empted the new minimalist approach.

FLORAL STILL LIFE
Flowers
Montbretia *(Crocosmia)*
Delphinium *(Delphinium)*
Agapanthus or 'African' lily *(Agapanthus africanus)*
'Nicole' rose *(Rosa* 'Nicole'*)*
Sweet William *(Dianthus barbatus)*
Anemone *(Anemone)*
Daffodil *(Narcissus)*
Lilac *(Syringa)*, Stock *(Matthiola)*
Gloriosa *(Gloriosa superba* 'Rothschildiana'*)*
Ranunculus *(Ranunculus)*
Lily-of-the-valley *(Convallaria majalis)*
Eucharis *(Eucharis grandiflora)*
'Blue moon' rose *(Rosa* 'Blue Moon'*)*
'Flaming Parrot' tulip *(Tulipa* 'Flaming Parrot'*)*
Crown imperial *(Fritillaria imperialis)*
Larkspur *(Delphinium consolida)*
Peony *(Paeonia)*
'Stirling Silver' rose *(Rosa* 'Stirling Silver'*)*
'Vicky Brown' rose *(Rosa* 'Vicky Brown'*)*
Scarlet plume *(Euphorbia fulgens)*
Amaryllis *(Hippeastrum)*
Broom *(Genista)*
Lisianthus *(Eustoma grandiflorum)*
Painter's palette *(Anthurium)*
'Paprika' achillea *(Achillea* 'Paprika'*)*
Fennel *(Foeniculum vulgare)*
Dill *(Anethum graveolens)*
Hyacinth *(Hyacinthus)*
Jonquil *(Narcissus* 'Jumblie'*)*
Marigold *(Calendula)*
Forget-me-not *(Myosotis)*
Mimosa *(Acacia)*
Polyanthus *(Primula)*
Silkweed *(Asclepias tuberosa)*
Foliage
Larch *(Larix)*
Rosemary *(Rosmarinus officinalis)*
Green pussy willow *(Salix caprea)*
Whitebeam *(Sorbus aria* 'Lutescens'*)*
Guelder rose *(Viburnum opulus)*

1 *It is best to attempt this kind of large-scale, exuberant arrangement which contains all sorts of different flowers at a time of year when many varieties are in season. This 17th-century still-life display contains many different blooms, and you may wish to make a more economical version by cutting down on the number of varieties. The first step is to condition all the cut flowers by leaving them to stand for several hours in nutrient-enriched water. (See Techniques page 174 for the treatment of different types of stems.) Place a bucket inside an urn, or any other suitable antique or reproduction period container – I have used a 19th-century iron urn. Take some large-mesh chicken wire and crumple it into a loose ball to fit inside the bucket. Pour water into the bucket. Wedge the bucket firmly into the urn with balls of crumpled paper, straw or moss so that it does not wobble. Start to establish the outline of the arrangement with the longest branches of foliage. Make sure that the tallest branches are at least one and a half times the height of the urn so that the overall display will look in proportion with the size of the container.*

2 *Add an assortment of the longer-stemmed flowers to the outline of foliage. There is no set rule of how, where and in what order you should arrange the plant material.*

3 *Continue to build up the density of the display with the large-headed flowers such as achilleas, delphiniums and lilac. Follow your own eye and subjectivity as you work; there is no right or wrong way to construct this arrangement.*

4 *Select shapely stems such as rosemary, broom, tulips and guelder rose to break any rigidity in the arrangement and give a feeling of movement. Add a few full-blown roses, tulips and a head of amaryllis to the middle of the display to draw the eye and act as the focal flowers. Full-blown flower heads are a feature of period floral paintings.*

5 *Fill in any remaining gaps with dill, fennel and smaller flowers such as forget-me-nots, hyacinths and jonquils.*

The final touch is to place a pineapple, a few figs and a single rose stem next to the urn to complete the still-life effect. The finished period arrangement is illustrated on the previous page.

MODERN THEMES

The 20th century has seen tremendous growth in the floristry industry and great developments in flower arranging as a hobby. The vogue for elegant parties and social functions at the beginning of the century called upon the skills of expert florists to decorate ballrooms, drawing rooms and hallways and so flower arranging became a recognized profession.

As early as 1900, in her book *Home and Garden*, author and floristry pioneer, Gertrude Jekyll, suggested using wire as an aid to flower arranging. But it was not until the 1930s that one of the most significant innovations in floristry took place: the marketing of crushed 50mm mesh wire. New wiring techniques were soon established, thus removing past limitations and allowing flowers to be arranged with far more versatility than ever before. During the 1950s flower arranging grew in popularity across Europe, partly as a reaction to the depression and deprivation of the post-war years. At a time when rationing reduced the luxuries of life, floral societies were a welcome institution and all sorts of materials were ingeniously used. Many women joined together to form flower-arranging clubs, inspired by demonstrations given by, for example, Violet Stevenson and Julia Clements. The latter, a prominent florist, toured the world teaching her skills, and, aware of the shortages of materials in a time when few vases and containers were manufactured and flowers were a rare commodity, she achieved remarkable results with tin cooking pans, gravy boats, chicken wire and garden flowers. In the 1960s, water-retaining florist's foam, which could hold stems at a desired angle, became the new, easy-to-use alternative to chicken wire. Together with moss, which was used to hide the mechanics of arrangements, foam extended the potential for flower arranging further.

The commercialization of floristry led to a so-called typical "English style" which developed during the 1950s. This style uses a variety of flowers and foliage massed together as if picked and mixed from a garden. The technical term for this kind of arrangement is "massed flowers" and these are then typically styled into a front-facing triangular form. Up until the 1970s the conventions of flower arranging were regarded as steadfast and the activity was generally rule-bound. Florists and flower arrangers tended to teach their skills according to prescribed methods – this is still largely the way that flower arranging is taught today. I am constantly amazed by students who regard correct technique to be more important than the overall visual effect of a display. Although I would be the first to argue that a sound knowledge of the fundamental principles of flower arranging is necessary before one can become too imaginative, I always urge people to follow their own eye.

As new frontiers in art, architecture and interior design were created, so flower arranging responded to these influences and changed too with the tide of the avant-garde. Contemporary sculpture in particular lent new dimensions and inspiration to flower arrangers and the established symmetrical, and very often triangular, shape of arrangements began to change, partly as a reaction to earlier strictures. New principles applied to modern flower arranging: colour, outline, shape and texture became all-important factors and the emphasis shifted away from the flowers themselves to focus on the actual process of arranging. There was now a place for the abstract, the unusual and the bizarre. When creating modern arrangements, I usually take my inspiration from tropical flowers for their strong colours, angles and forms. However, country, woodland and seaside walks often provide rich hunting grounds for materials such as fungi, twigs, and weathered stones and wood. What makes modern flower arranging exciting is that any plant material with an interesting form can be employed and there is no such thing as the incongruous. Ribbons, rope, paper and other inorganic materials can also be used.

Modern arrangements are particularly suitable for livening up functional environments, such as offices and reception areas where colours are usually neutral and furniture uninspiring. Because modern themes tend to be minimalist and unfussy, the clean lines of the design should be given maximum impact. For this reason space and a plain background are important – the latter will highlight the colours and forms in the arrangement and the overall effect will be enhanced by leaving space around the flower heads as well as in-between the various elements making up the arrangement. You can create successful modern arrangements in monochromatic or bright colour schemes. It is best to select flowers with strong shapes such as birds of paradise (*Strelitzia reginae*), painter's palettes (*Anthurium*) and orchids. Large-headed flowers such as these are often costly but they should be used sparingly to give them prominence. The precepts behind modern flower arranging are very different to those used when creating traditional arrangements. You should choose flowers with defined outlines which are preferably strong in colour, and foliage should not be treated as an infill for gaps, but should stand for itself.

The Japanese art of flower arranging, or ikebana, has contributed to modern arranging throughout the world. Ikebana is generally made from living plant material and is heavily loaded with religious and philosophical symbolism. Traditionally it has been taught and passed down the generations by men. As Japanese interiors tend to be sparsely furnished, ikebana provides a focus to interior settings and is designed to capture the eye, the mind and the senses. It aims to create a powerful impact and great care is taken in the planning of an arrangement. Lines rather than colours are the visual priority and the arrangement should always be set against a plain background or a screen. All sorts of unlikely materials can be used: pieces of gnarled driftwood, knots of vine, branches of blossom, split bamboo, contorted willow, reeds, withered branches or twigs which are often painted or gilded, and pieces of metal, stone, slate, plastic and glass.

Recently, florists have tended to make greater use of dried flowers when creating modern designs, which fall into the category of "living" sculptures. Moss, pine cones, yarrow heads (*Achillea millefolium*), hogweed (*Heracleum sphondylium*) and a variety of dried twigs such as birch (*Betula*) and larch (*Larix*) all make interesting sculptural shapes. All sorts of materials now find their way into contemporary floral designs: dried flowers such as hydrangea heads (*Hydrangea macophylla*) fruits, vegetables and nuts, wheat, artichokes (*Cynara scolymus*), poppy (*Papaver*) seedheads and fir cones. These are bound into wreaths, drops and collages of all shapes and sizes. Decorator Kenneth Turner developed the idea of floral collage to almost surreal proportions. His work includes arrangements of sea flowers such as corals, shells and sponges and his famous "wall trophies". These displays of flowers, foliage, bunches of grapes and baskets of fruits and vegetables are arranged around terracotta pots and life-sized gardening equipment such as wheelbarrows, rakes, hoes and watering cans. His floral assemblages demonstrate that there is still room for ingenuity in the age-old art of flower-arranging.

MINIMAL COMPOSITION

1 *First condition the heliconias, leaving them to stand in water for several hours. (Heliconias are available in pink, red and orange varieties, so you can choose a particular colour to match a setting.) Then select a suitable plain container. I have used a white-washed beehive terra-cotta urn from the Philippines. If you choose an unglazed vase of this sort it will not be waterproof, so a smaller, watertight container, such as a glass cylinder, must be placed inside it to hold the stems.*

2 *Crumple some large-gauge chicken or mesh wire into a loose ball to fit inside the inner glass container. Fill the glass cylinder with water. (It is better to use large-gauge chicken wire as you will find it easier to insert the stems.)*

Flowers
Ginger heliconia *(Heliconia)*
Foliage
Tortured willow
(Salix matsudana 'Tortuosa')
or: Contorted hazel
(Corylus avellana 'Contorta')

3 *Establish the outline of the arrangement with tortured willow. You can also use contorted hazel. If you are unable to obtain dried twigs, then you can take green willow twigs and strip off the outer bark so that they are brown.*

4 *Once you have arranged the willow or hazel twigs add the long stems of ginger heliconia, distributing the red heads of the flowers evenly in-between the willow. Because of the sparsity of the plant material you may be tempted to overfill the container; avoid doing this as the idea is to create a minimal feel.*

Leave space around each of the heliconia heads and in-between the willow branches so that the plant material is given maximum visual impact. Break a few short pieces of willow and arrange them around the mouth of the container in order to hide the mechanics of the chicken wire. Set the container against a plain background. The finished modern arrangement is illustrated on the previous page.

SIMPLE THEMES

The overall effect of any simple arrangement should be that the flowers and foliage look natural without being over-arranged, over-wired or too symmetrical. A single flower, perhaps with a sprig of foliage, in a specimen vase is an instant way to create the ultimate simple arrangement. When you are using a small number of stems it is especially important to choose flowers in prime condition as the second-rate won't escape notice. Roses *(Rosa)* stand well singly and just a few heads of any variety of lily *(Lilium)* make a striking display and look best when arranged in an understated fashion, without being cluttered by other flowers or foliage. For something less grandiose you can take a bunch of cottage scabious *(Scabiosa)* or poppies *(Papaver)* and let them fall in a loose spray in a vase. Making simple arrangements from just one type of flower offers a good opportunity to use stems which fade fast. Mixed together, short-lived flowers will poison other types of longer-lasting flowers and cause them to die prematurely.

Another idea that has been envisonaged by informalist and interior designer David Hicks is to fill a glass, square-shaped container with tulip heads, after having cut their stems to an equal length. With the flower heads bunched close together, the effect is one of a miniature "field" of tulips. Some of my favourite flowers for arranging naturally and randomly in a vase are gloriosas *(Gloriosa)*, arum lilies *(Zantedeschia)*, 'Casablanca' lilies *(Lilium 'Casablanca')*, tulips, gerberas *(Gerbera)*, anemones *(Anemone)*, heliconias *(Heliconia)*, painter's palettes *(Anthurium)*, montbretia *(Crocosmia)* and thistiles *(Carlina)*. The secret to simple arranging is to consider the natural characteristics of the flowers themselves. Their colours, shapes and the strength and shape of their stems will determine the container you use and how you can arrange them for maximum effect. For example, drooping Parrot tulips look their best when no attempt is made to curb their curving stems and they are left to hang over the edge of a rounded vase, while spiky Aladdin tulips are much better suited to display in an upright vase.

I prefer to use a minimum of artificial aids when working to a simple theme as artifice contradicts the overall aim. If the stems don't fall in an even symmetry so much the better, as the idea is to appreciate the simplicity and naturalness of the end result. Nevertheless, in many cases arrangements do need certain mechanics to give them stability and provide balance both in terms of weight and visually and it *is* possible to secure flowers in a container simply without having to rely on chicken wire or foam. The first step is to find a container with a low centre of gravity so that the arrangement will not topple over. Then you can take twigs such as tortured willow *(Salix matsudana* 'Tortuosa'), contorted hazel *(Corylus avellana* 'Contorta'), dogwood *(Cornus)*, birch *(Betula)* or any sorts of twigs with seasonal catkins, buds, blossom or blooming foliage. Among my favourite decorative twigs are pussy willow *(Salix caprea)*, berry-laded cotoneaster *(Cotoneaster)*, the mauve-berried callicarpa *(Callicarpa)* and whitebeam *(Sorbus aria)*. If you use twigs as a framework to a simple arrangement the ends of the stems will naturally overlap inside the container and form a woody cradle which provides a perfectly good substitute to chicken wire. In the same way you can arrange flowers so that their stems cross over and support each other inside a vase and so dispense with the need for mechanics. You should cut some of the stems short to give the whole arrangement stability, as short stems will help the display maintain a low centre of gravity.

A very attractive way to arrange stems inside glass containers is to spiral them in your hand in the same way that a "continental tied bunch" is put together. This method is especially suited to fishbowls and round containers and after a little practice you will find the procedure quick and easy. The first step in making such a hand-tied bunch is to strip any leaves off the stems that will be below the water line. Take the longest stem first – this should be a striking focal flower for the middle of the bunch. Hold it in your left hand if right-handed, and vice versa if left-handed, and form a ring of flowers around it. Turn the bunch in your hand as you do this so that you build up a spiralling effect of stems. It is very important to keep your hand relaxed as the arrangement will start to look more formal if you hold the flowers too tightly. You can bind the stems together with green raffia or string and if you wish the binding can be left on in the vase, although I normally cut mine to let the flowers fall more freely. If the stems are sufficiently spiralled you should be able to remove the flowers to change the water and the bunch should stay intact when replaced. Balanced correctly, this kind of bunch will hold together well and looks like a sheaf of corn. This technique is illustrated as a step–by–step method on page 175.

For novice flower arrangers and those short of time, flower heads can be floated in a bowl of water. Pebbles, shells and small floating candles will all add to the effect. Scented blooms such as the flower of the hoya *(Hoya)* plant are particularly effective for this treatment because when floated on water along with bobbing candles the heat from the flames will bring out their perfume. The bold-coloured heads of gerberas *(Gerbera)* and the lavish purple, white and pink cups of lotus *(Nelumbo)* flowers are also ideal for floating in shallow containers. Another quick and easy way to create a stunning simple group of flowers is to place three vases of differing heights together and fill each one with flowers of the same colour. For example, one vase can be filled with red amaryllis *(Hippeastrum)*, a second with two red tulips *(Tulipa)* and a third with a bunch of red berries.

The aim of any arrangement is to produce a harmonious union between flowers and foliage and the container that is to hold them. Some of the skill involved in getting this right is intuitive but some can be learned. To keep an arrangement looking simple try to use the foliage from the stems of your chosen flowers rather than adding too much extraneous foliage. You must remove any leaves that will be below the waterline in the container as these will rot quickly and may contaminate the water with bacteria and so reduce the longevity of the flowers. However, you should leave as much leaf as possible above the rim of the container to make the flowers look natural.

One other simple way to arrange flowers is the so-called "parallel" style that is often adopted in European countries and which is particularly popular with the Dutch. The method behind this type of arrangement involves taking a block of florist's foam and placing flower stems into it so that they cover the whole surface area of the foam. This means that the stems have a widespread base and do not radiate from a central point as is so characteristic of the traditional "massed" style. By inserting stems over a larger surface area you can build up zones of colours and groups of flowers, interspersing them with foliage to create an almost planted effect. This "vegetative" style tries to imitate the way that flowers grow in their natural habitats and avoids the concept of focal flowers in favour of providing an even distribution of plant material. So, the arrangement aspires to be a naturalistic reflection of the simplicity of growing flowers.

ONE-COLOUR ARRANGEMENT

1 *The first step is to condition the crown imperials: make a fresh cut at the base of the stem, on an angle, so that the flowers can drink easily. Then place the stems in a bucket of nutrient-enriched water for several hours. In the meantime prepare the rest of the material for the arrangement. Take a yellow star fruit which is not too ripe; if it is too soft it will not cut cleanly and will rot quickly. Cut across the width of the fruit with a sharp knife, so that the pieces are star-shaped. Take the yellow craspedias and remove the flower heads or "balls" from the stems. I have used a glass fish bowl for this arrangement, but you can choose an alternative container, providing it is glass, as the idea is to make a feature of the container as well as the flowers themselves. Start to line the inside of the fish bowl with bun moss, working from the bottom of the container upward. Make a pattern so that the slices of star fruit and craspedia heads are surrounded by moss, and continue to line the sides of the bowl. Because the container is curved, you will have to use a padding of moss inside the bowl to prevent the "lining" from slipping. Leave a space in the middle for a flat-based glass cylinder to stand.*

2 *Continue to build up the lining of moss, slices of star fruit and craspedia heads until you have covered the whole of the inside of the bowl. Before you reach*

Flowers
Craspedia *(Craspedia globosa)*
Crown imperial *(Fritillaria imperialis)*
Foliage
Bear grass *(Dasylirion)*
Bun moss
Fruit
Star fruit *(Averrhoa carambola)*

the rim of the fish bowl, place the glass cylinder inside it, making sure that the inner glass container fits the outer bowl and that the rims of both vessels are almost level.

3 *Fill in the space in-between the outside of the inner cylinder and the inside of the outer bowl using more moss and some small stones or pebbles for extra bulk. Make sure that the stones are hidden and that the craspedia heads and slices of star fruit are evenly distributed. Then fill the inner glass cylinder with water. Take some long strands of bear grass and tie them together at one end, fixing this knotted end to a hook or door knob so that you have both hands free to make a plait. Take care not to cut your hands on the grass as the blades are sharp. Then fix the plait of grass around the rim of the bowl and knot the two*

ends together at the back. Once your container is prepared, take the crown imperials and strip away any leaves lower down on the stems as these will make the water turn green and encourage the growth of bacteria, so reducing the longevity of the flowers. Make sure that you leave the foliage on the upper stems as it will add to the overall effect. The stems of crown imperials curve naturally toward the light, giving shape and movement to the arrangement. The finished simple arrangement is illustrated on the previous page.

The success of this arrangement depends on its one-colour theme, which is all the more strikingly simple because only one type of flower has been used. You can create all sorts of variations on this theme, taking for example any variety of red or orange lilies and arranging them in the same way. You can decorate a glass container by matching the colours of the cut flowers with fruits, for example: cherries (Prunus avium); ornamental hot or chili peppers (Capsicum frutescens); hard red berries such as barberries (Berberis), sea buckthorn (Hippophae rhamnoides) and cranberries (Vaccinium); pitangas or Surinam cherries (Eugenia uniflora); the small orange fruits of Chinese lanterns or Cape gooseberries (Physalis) or perhaps the knobbly red lychee (Litchi chinensis).

FORMAL THEMES

In some respects the commercialization of floristy has led to flower shops producing arrangements which lack creativity and spontaneity. All too often, trained florists arrange flowers according to a formula, using scant foliage so that the results are devoid of natural grace and form. The standard of arranging flowers in a front-facing, triangular shape has been adopted all over the world, in particular by the relay flower business. For this reason I steer away from this formula which has narrowed the public's concept of what formal flower arranging can be about. Formal arrangements can be created by using plant material in a structured, symmetrical way and context is all-important. For example, a pair of loosely arranged pedestals will look formal placed either side of a chancel or next to an altar in a church. It is currently fashionable to arrange fresh flowers with dried material such as lavender *(Lavandula)* and wheat *(Triticum aestirium)* so that all the plant material is of the same height – a simple approach which gives the arrangement a formal effect.

The art of floristry should be individual to the extent that no two florists arrange in exactly the same way with identical results. With an ever-expanding flower industry there is a danger that commercial demands will make floristry more and more stereotyped, leaving little room for innovation. I try and encourage people to look upon flowers as they might regard food; the methodology of cooking varies enormously, and something as simple as an omelette can be presented in all sorts of guises. In the same way the basic ingredients of flower arranging may be standard, but the ways of using and inter-relating the materials are limitless.

Formal arrangements are especially suited to public places such as hotel lobbies, corporate entrance halls and religious buildings and to occasions like parties and celebrations. They often require a considerable amount of plant material in order to create a strong impact, and because of their scale a larger budget than usual may be involved. There are a few tips which will help when tackling this kind of flower arranging. First, if you are planning to decorate a special setting such as a church, a function room or a marquee you should visit the location at least once and get a clear idea of the space you are aiming to fill, the scale of the interior and any particular features such as electric wires, beams, areas which need free access and prime spots where your arrangements should be positioned. Second, if a large number of people are expected to attend the function you will have to place flowers above shoulder height so that they are visible. Third, it is important to take lighting into consideration as this will affect the impact of the display. If the setting is dark or candlelit choose lightly coloured flowers, as blues, greens and purples will be lost. Your arrangement will be highlighted if lit from in front or above, and will gain nothing if lit from behind. Finally, do not worry if you cannot obtain large containers necessary for creating sizeable arrangements as ordinary buckets are quite adequate and can always be disguised with moss and foliage. You will probably be working to a considerable budget if you are decorating a large space, but it will nevertheless *be* a budget so you should take care of your material. It is important to separate the different plant material into buckets of water – not only because formal arranging tends to be time-consuming and the flowers will suffer if they get thirsty, but also because laying flowers down on a surface may damage the blooms.

The lavish canvases of the great Dutch and Flemish flower painters such as Jan Bruegel and Jan Vermeer van Delft offer plenty of inspiration for formal themes. Although these arrangements, with their unlikely and extravagant mixtures of full-blown blooms, myriad colours and swirling foliage, are not true representations of Nature, the detail and grandeur of the compositions offer a rich source of ideas. The particularly decorative flowers such as narcissi *(Narcissus)*, irises *(Iris)*, anemones *(Anemone)* and peonies *(Paeonia)* that were depicted in these paintings are all suitable for recreating grand period displays. However, I would recommend that instead of using too many varieties, as artistic licence allowed these genre painters to do, you limit the number you include in a formal arrangement to between half a dozen and a dozen types of flowers and foliage.

The archetypal formal theme is the pedestal arrangement. Pedestals are used primarily to raise flowers to eye-level so that they are given maximum impact. Your pedestal should always have a sturdy base to support the considerable weight of the mechanics, water and plant material. Secure a wide-mouthed container to the top of the pedestal using strong reel wire and tape and then fill it either with florist's foam or with loosely crumpled chicken wire and water. This second alternative has the advantage that the stems will be able to drink more freely and the arrangement will consequently last better. A typical pedestal arrangement is front-facing and relies on an outline of foliage, twigs in blossom or tall flowers such as delphiniums *(Delphinium)*, stocks *(Matthiola)*, lupins *(Lupinus)* and foxgloves *(Digitalis)*. Foliage such as laurel *(Laurellia)* and rhododendron *(Euonymus japonicus)* and trailing ivy *(Hedera)*, infilled with flat or bushy leaves such as hosta *(Hosta)*, sea lavender *(Limonium)* and fern, are ideal for hiding the unslightly mechanics around the mouth of the container. Once you have established your outline, complete the arrangement with large, showy flowers.

Another way to achieve large-scale formal displays is to use a tiered structure similar to an over-sized *épergne*. During the 19th century *épergnes* – originally designed to hold fruit – were adapted to carry flowers and foliage in a cascade of plant material. Hostesses in the 19th century were so keen to impress that some even went as far as carving a hole in the middle of the dining-room table to allow palms and fronds to grow up from the floor and fountain over the table in a mass of lush greenery! Without ruining your dining-room table, you can build impressive pyramid arrangements by putting wet florist's foam into a stable, bottom-heavy container and covering the foam with chicken wire. Then add fruit, vegetables and flowers to the pyramid so that all the foam is covered. If you spray the arrangement with water it will remain fresh and colourful on a buffet table.

Another formal theme I enjoy working to is the topiary tree. Topiary involves not simply arranging flowers but actually sculpting plant material into stylized shapes. This dimension of flower arranging is currently in fashion and the topiary form offers all sorts of decorative possibilities using dried or fresh flowers and leaves. Your starting point should be a flat-based pot which is filled with plaster of Paris, quick-drying cement or better still dry-hard clay (be careful with the former as it expands as it dries and may crack a fragile container). Place a sturdy piece of wood – perhaps a small branch picked up on a country walk – vertically into the pot and hold it upright until the mixture has set. Then wire blocks of foam around the top of the "trunk" and create the "tree" – you can add lavender *(Lavandula)*, dried yellow curry plant *(Helichrysum angustifolium)*, box leaf *(Buxus)*, lichen, moss or any sort of evergreen foliage, as well as fruits and flowers.

CLASSICAL GRANDEUR

1 *The first step is to condition your flowers by leaving them in a bucketful of nutrient-enriched water for several hours. Place a bucket inside a heavy urn and wedge it in firmly so that the container is stable and can support a large amount of plant material. This reconstituted marble urn was bought new and made to look antique by rubbing gray and brown emulsion or latex paint into the stone with an old rag, and flicking and brushing paint into the crevices with an old toothbrush. Take some large-gauge chicken or mesh wire (this makes inserting the stems easier) and loosely crumple it into a ball to fit inside the bucket.*

2 *This is a large arrangement and the finished display measured at least 6.5ft (2m) in height once it was finished. Most formal displays should be large-scale and placed at, or above, eye level in order to be noticed. You should select plant material with long stems to give the arrangement height; you can also use plastic florist's cones or tubes as a tool for lengthening stems (see Techniques, pages 172-3). Attach several cones to ordinary garden canes (which can be broken to the required length), securing them with wire and tape before placing them at different angles into the chicken wire.*

Flowers
Agapanthus or 'African' lily *(Agapanthus africanus)*
Foxtail lily *(Eremurus)*
'Casablanca' lily *(Lilium* 'Casablanca'*)*
Chimney bellflower
(Campanula pyramidalis)
Delphinium *(Delphinium)*
Onion head *(Allium giganteum)*
Amaryllis *(Hippeastrum)*
Arum lily *(Zantedeschia aethiopica)*
Foliage
Flowering privet *(Ligustrum)*
Variegated ivy *(Hedera)*
Snowberry *(Symphoricarpos albus)*
Miniature date palm *(Phoenix roebelenii)*
Plants
Two potted hydrangeas *(Hydrangea macrophylla)*

3 *Take the flowering privet and the large fronds of date palm to establish the outline of the arrangement, and place swags of trailing ivy over the rim of the urn. Above all, don't be afraid to make the outline large. It is better to be bold at the beginning than to*

get halfway through an arrangement before you realize that the display is too small and to have to begin again. The plant material must be in proportion with the size of the urn; as a general guideline, the arrangement should be at least one and a half times the height of the container.

4 *Arrange the longer-stemmed flowers such as the delphiniums and the agapanthus.*

5 *Next add the snowberries and onion heads.*

6 *Place the short-stemmed flowers such as the chimney bellflowers and the arum lilies into the cones. Take two potted hydrangeas and insert two or three canes through the holes in the bottom of the flower pots. If there are no holes in the base of the pots then remove them completely and insert the canes directly into the peat moss itself. Place the canes supporting the hydrangeas into the middle of the arrangement, so that their large heads will act as the focal flowers. Add the hollow-stemmed amaryllis. Insert canes into their stems to prevent them from drooping (see Techniques, page 177). Fill in any gaps with Foxtail and 'Casablanca' lilies and make sure that the display has an even density throughout. The finished formal arrangement is illustrated on the previous page.*

COUNTRY BASKET

1 *If you grow flowers in your garden then you already have an ideal source of material for making informal arrangements. When you pick blooms straight from the garden, you must always give them a long drink of nutrient-enriched water before you start arranging, otherwise they will soon begin to wilt and look tired. (All cut flowers will look fresher for longer if they have been properly conditioned before arranging.) You should avoid wiring any plant material when creating an informal theme; instead allow the stems and flower heads to fall naturally. Seasonal blossom as well as all kinds of flowering foliage and herbs are suitable for informal arranging. Place a bucket inside a plain container, I used a 19th-century bran tub. You can choose a simple earthenware pot or a terra-cotta vase, or perhaps a basket or wooden trug to arrange in. If the container you choose is not watertight you must place a bucket or a waterproof receptacle inside it. Take some large-mesh chicken wire (this makes inserting the stems easier than a small mesh) and crumple it into a loose ball so that it fits inside the bucket. Then fill the bucket with water. You should wedge the bucket inside the outer container with crumpled paper, straw or moss.*

Flowers
Dill *(Anethum graveolens)*, Marjoram *(Origanum)*
Masterwort *(Astrantia)*, Soapwort *(Saponaria)*
Poppy *(Papaver)*
Love-lies-bleeding *(Amaranthus caudatus)*
Globe artichoke *(Cynara scolymus)*
Lupin *(Lupinus)*, Stock *(Matthiola)*
Cow parsley *(Anthriscus sylvestris)*
Mullein *(Verbascum)*
Mock orange *(Philadelphus coronarius)*
Valerian *(Valeriana)*
Cirsium *(Cirsium)*
Eupatorium *(Eupatorium)*
Mallow *(Malva)*, Scabious *(Scabiosa)*
Milkweed *(Euphorbia)*
Achillea *(Achillea)*
Phlomis *(Phlomis)*
Loosestrife *(Lysimachia)*

Foliage
Dock seedhead *(Rumex)*
Oats *(Avena sativa)*, Millet *(Millum)*
Rue *(Ruta graveolens)*
Copper beech *(Fagus sylvatica purpurea)*
Giant reeds and ornamental grass *(Arundo donax)*
'August Moon' Hosta *(Hosta* 'August Moon')

2 *Select a handful of various different foliages and place them grouped together into the container. Although the taller grasses and dock seedheads will be eye-catching, some of the smaller grasses will look flimsy and will hardly be visible unless you bunch them together into a sheaf to give them as much visual impact as possible.*

3 *Establish the outline of the arrangement with the white flowers such as soapwort, mallow, masterwort, cow parsley and mock orange. There is no right or wrong way about how and where you should place your flowers; this should be a matter of instinct and subjectivity, so follow your own eye. The whole arrangement should look spontaneous rather than contrived, so be careful not to over-arrange the plant material.*

4 *Continue to fill in any gaps with flowers of different colours and make sure that all the flower heads are facing forward. You must singe the ends of the poppy stems before adding them to the foam (see Techniques, page 174) otherwise they contaminate the water. Use the hanging love-lies-bleeding and the masterwort to give the display shape and movement. The finished informal arrangement is illustrated on the previous page.*

TROPICAL THEMES

In the same way that the 19th-century plant collectors of the Western world delighted in exotic flowers and plants which were discovered in unexplored corners of the globe, so today's flower-buying public in Europe and America enjoy the novelty of tropical flowers. Improved means of transportation of flowers by air, and better packaging, mean that tropical flowers from all sorts of far-flung places can arrive daily to wherever there is a market for them. As a general rule, because such flowers thrive naturally in hot and humid climates they tend also to be fairly resilient and I often recommend them because they are long-lasting. Despite being comparatively expensive out of their natural habitat their longevity means that they are in fact good value. However, the main disadvantage of tropical flowers is that they do not wither, fade and gently dry out as do traditional temperate climate garden flowers. Instead of declining gracefully and gradually, they will suddenly turn black and rotten.

Arranging tropical flowers is an exciting exercise because of their strong colours and elaborate forms. I feel that there is really no such thing as flowers which clash since in the wild you find all sorts of hues growing naturally alongside each other. For some reason, people tend to be bolder with colours when arranging naturally vibrant tropical flowers. If you want to tone colours down in an arrangement you can always use plenty of lush tropical foliage such as palm fronds or ferns. One essential tip to bear in mind is that out of their natural habitat tropical flowers need to be kept away from drafts and in fairly warm temperatures. They have an almost human reaction to cold and will start to look blue and eventually turn black and die. You will need a strong pair of secateurs to cut their stems after transit and they should then be conditioned in a bucketful of warm, nutrient-rich water. The freight boxes which arrive in my shop from the Windward Islands in the West Indies come with hand-written notes from the growers, who suggest that the flowers will last better in water with added sugar or lemonade, whereas tropical flowers grown in high-tech, centrally heated glass houses in the Netherlands are supplied with a special solution which will revive them after transportation.

As the world becomes ever more multicultural, it must be a welcome sight for South Africans to see their national flower, the king protea *(Protea)*, for West Indians to see the painter's palette *(Anthurium)* and for Australians and Californians to see birds of paradise *(Strelitzia reginae)* in florist shops far from home, although they may well be amazed at the cost of such flowers which grow so profusely on their native soil. It is a nice touch that international companies often pay tribute to their country of origin by displaying flowers native to that country in overseas offices.

South Africa offers the world flower market a tremendous variety of flowers. Proteas, most of which are cultivated for export in Cape Province, although they are also grown commercially in Madeira and Hawaii, are long-lasting and also dry well. They have very thick stems and like all cut flowers they will live longer if arranged in water rather than in florist's foam. In fact, they drink so much that they will not survive for long in foam. South Africa is also the home of many other plants which are familiar worldwide: nerines *(Nerine)*, African Lilies *(Agapanthus africanus)*, arum lilies *(Zantedeschia)*, Belladonna lilies *(Amaryllis belladonna)*, and common houseplants such as the prayer plant *(Maranta)*, monstera *(Montsera)*, croton *(Codiaeum variegatum)* and the ubiquitous yucca *(Yucca)*.

Mexico is a country with a rich botanical history and popular native plants such as echeverias *(Echeveria)*, the colourful zinnias *(Zinnia)*, fuschias *(Fuschia)*, begonias *(Begonia)* and one of the world's best-loved plants, the poinsettia *(Euphorbia pulcherrima)*. Its popularity dates from an exhibition in Pennsylvania in 1829, where it was first brought into the public eye. Poinsettias are happiest in warm climates and you may have noticed that they all too often suffer from drafts and cold weather. Another native flower of Mexico, and one of my favourites, is the scarlet plume *(Euphorbia fulgens)*. It comes in a variety of colours and is ideal for arranging because of its tendency to curve. It is worth mentioning here that all the flowers in this family omit a sticky, milky sap from their stems which is an irritant to the skin. Snow-on-the-mountain *(Euphorbia marginata)* is especially virulent, so take care to wash your hands thoroughly after handling any species of spurge *(Euphorbia)*.

The Caribbean Islands are another source of tropical inspiration, with their heliconias *(Heliconia)*, oleanders *(Nerium oleander)* and hibiscus *(Hibiscus)*. It is interesting to note that florists in this part of the world import gladioli *(Gladiolus)* and all sorts of roses *(Rosa)* for their novelty value. My favourite Caribbean flower is celosia *(Celosia)*, which has rich, jewel-like colours and a velvety texture. People often think this is a brand new variety, but in fact celosia seeds have been found among the mummified remains in Egyptian tombs.

Australia also has its own unique flora, many of which are now exported to flower markets across the world. One of my favourite flowers native to Australia is kangeroo paw *(Anigozanthos)*, which incidentally is also grown in Israel. This small family of flowers comes in the most unusual colours and, as the name suggests, they have a furry texture. The dark-red variety is a stunning flower to use at Christmas time, especially if you mix it with holly *(Ilex)* berries and amaryllis *(Hippeastrum)*. Hanging amaranthus *(Amaranthus caudatus)*, which also grows wild in Australia, looks very good in garlands, giving a room a rich, festive and very 19th-century feel.

Colombia is another important flower-producing country. While most of its fine flowers are flown to nearby North America, some, such as the colourful painter's palette *(Anthurium)* are being sent to Europe. These are long-lasting and look effective on their own or in a massed display. What we think of as the flower is really the showy *spathe* or large bract, while the flower is actually the less colourful *spadix* or spike of clustered flowers in the middle of the "palette".

Tropical arrangements allow you to let your imagination run riot. You can combine all sorts of bright colours and add accessories such as fruits, vegetables, coconuts, shells, stones, bamboo, bark, driftwood, rope, raffia and even swathes of vivid fabric to your arrangements. Although most Europeans and North Americans will find that imported tropical flowers are expensive, a few stems will be enough to catch the eye and you can always supplement them with inexpensive houseplants such as cacti or cycas *(Cycas)*, as well as all sorts of jungly foliage to good effect.

VIBRANT TABLESCAPE

1 *First condition all the cut flowers by leaving them to stand in a bucket of nutrient-enriched water for several hours. You will need a large surface to work on. Take a quantity of moss and shape it into a "sausage". Take a reel of wire and wind it around the moss. Add another layer of moss and bind this with more reel wire. Build up the thickness of the moss base in this way until it is the size and shape you require. Surround the moss with large-mesh chicken wire and bind it all together with reel wire. This arrangement was about 4 ft (1.5 m) in length. I suggest that you arrange a large tropical tablescape in situ and protect the table with a sheet of cellophane or plastic film. Next, take some blocks of wet florist's foam and round off the square edges with a sharp knife – this makes it easier to insert the flower stems. Secure the foam into the moss using a piece of stub wire bent into a hairpin shape. Wire and tape 1 ft (30 cm) lengths of fresh green bamboo diagonally across the moss base so that they are butting up against the foam.*

2 *Take some lengths of any brightly coloured fabric which matches the colours of your flowers and spiral them around the moss base. I used mustard and magenta raw silk to complement the plant material.*

Flowers
'Eoliet' gerbera *(Gerbera* 'Eoilet')
Hydrangea *(Hydrangea macrophylla)*
Gloriosa *(Gloriosa superba* 'Rothschildiana')
Ornamental pineapple *(Ananas comosus)*
Belladonna lily *(Amaryllis belladonna)*
'La Reve' lily *(Lilium* 'La Reve')
Arum lily *(Zantedeschia)*
Protea *(Protea repens)*
Celosia *(Celosia argentea)*
Joe Pye weed *(Eupatorium purpureum)*
Heliconia *(Heliconia)*

Foliage
Aralia *(Aralia)*
Bamboo

Fruit
Miniature pineapple *(Ananas comosus)*
Miniature aubergine *(Solanum)*
Custard apple *(Annona squamosa)*
Star fruit *(Averrhoa carambola)*
Miniature banana *(Musa paradisiaca)*

Vegetables
Kohl-rabi *(Brassica oleracea gongylodes)*
Miniature red cabbage
(Brassica oleracea capitata alba)

3 *Place aralia leaves all around the base of the arrangement. Wipe the leaves with a damp cloth if they are dusty.*

4 *Take some miniature red cabbages and cut them in half to show their frilly interiors. Attach these with a piece of stub wire bent into a hairpin shape (see Techniques, page 177). Then wire the miniature aubergines, the custard apples, miniature pineapples and star fruit in the same way and insert them into the moss base.*

5 *Cut the stems off the celosias and group together red, pink and yellow flower heads into a fan shape. Wire these onto the moss base. Cut the stems of the magenta gerberas short and insert them, with the ornamental pink pineapples, into the foam. Place the heliconias and the miniature pineapples in the middle of the arrangement.*

6 *Add the Belladonna lilies, the small pink arum lilies and the gloriosas, inserting the stems straight into the foam. Leave the hollow ends of the bamboo visible and make sure that all the mechanics are hidden. Cut away the cellophane or plastic film, trimming it as close to the moss base as possible. The finished tropical arrangement is illustrated on the previous page.*

SCENTED THEMES

Flowers, leaves, roots and barks have scented our homes, clothes and surroundings for thousands of years. The origin of the word "perfume", which derives from *per fumin* and translates as "by means of smoke", suggests that the scented properties of plants were first realized when wood, sticks and stems were burned and released aromatic smoke. For many people the appreciation of flowers lies as much in their distinctive scents as in their individual colours and shapes. Flowers omit a smell primarily in order to attract insects which assist in pollination. However, some plants such as wormwood (*Artemisia*) have acrid-smelling leaves as a deterrent to insects and herbivorous animals, and others such as ornamental onion heads (*Allium aflatunense*) and crown imperials (*Fritillaria imperialis*) let off a pungent odour when damaged or bruised. The sweet smells of garden flowers such as buddleias (*Buddleia*), wallflowers (*Cheiranthus*), tuberoses (*Polianthes tuberosa*), foxgloves (*Digitalis*) and mock orange (*Philadelphus coronarius*) are particularly strong on a hot day and by nightfall the heady fragrances brought out by hours sunshine can be overpowering. If cut flowers are kept in a very cold room they will lose their scent; a warm room will have the opposite effect and brings out their full perfume, although too warm a temperature will precipitate wilting. Some of the more showy flowers, for example hollyhocks (*Alcea*), sunflowers (*Helianthus*) and zinnias (*Zinnia*), have little fragrance and rely instead on their flamboyant colours to attract pollinators. At the other end of the scale, small flowers such as violets (*Viola odorata*), freesias (*Freesia*) and pinks (*Dianthus*) compensate for their size by exuding an intense perfume.

Many of today's sweet-smelling varieties — pinks (*Dianthus plumarius*), sweet William (*Dianthus barbatus*), stocks (*Matthiola*) and lavender (*Lavandula*) — were being cultivated during the Middle Ages for the practical purposes they played in domestic life. For example, lavender, whose name originates from the Latin meaning "to wash", was dried in bunches and folded into linen, giving laundry a clean, astringent smell. There are over 25 varieties of lavender, with flowers in pink and white as well as the more common purple. The large flowering variety from France (*Lavandula stoechas*) has a deep colouring and adds zest to arrangments. All sorts of herbs and flowers, including juniper (*Juniperus*), woodruff (*Asperula odorata*) and meadowsweet (*Filipendula*), as well as bracken and rushes, were strewn inside houses to take the chill off stone floors and conceal household dirt. During medieval times when hygiene was minimal, scent was held as something almost magical and two flowers in particular were revered for their fragrance. The hallowed Madonna lily (*Lilium candidum*), with its white trumpet-shaped flowers, was a medieval symbol of purity and spirituality. The more commonly grown and therefore less expensive variety, the Easter lily (*Lilium longiflorum*), is still an adornment of altars throughout the world. Lilies in general not only exude a heavenly smell but last well if bought when the buds are still closed and the petals are turning from green to white. They should also be kept cool.

The vast majority of flowers sold today are grown commercially and as colour and longevity are considered all-important scent has been undermined through intensive cross-breeding, a fact which is especially true of roses. Fortunately, there is now a growing demand for fragrant blooms as well as flowers which impress because they are in peak condition. In general, white and pale flowers are heavily scented, such as all sorts of lilies (*Lilium*), white carnations (*Dianthus*), narcissi (*Narcissus tazetta*), honeysuckle (*Lonicera*), lily-of-the-valley (*Convallaria majalis*), gardenias (*Gardenia*), stephanotis (*Stephanotis*) and sweet peas (*Lathyrus odoratus*). With sweet peas, you will find that the florist's variety are considerably longer lasting than those picked straight from the garden, and you should change their water daily to increase longevity.

Herbs offer a host of scents which will enliven fresh or dried flower arrangements. Some varieties, such as the bright yellow seedheads of fennel (*Foeniculum vulgare*), the umbrella-shaped flowers of dill (*Anethum graveolens*) and the button-like flowers of cotton lavender (*Santolina chamaecyparissus*), can be massed together to make an attractive herbal bunch. You can dry herbs and flowers simply by hanging them upside down in a warm place. The warmer the air is around them the faster they will dry out and the more colour they will retain. Scent often fades with drying, but a few drops of an essential oil derived from the same flower will revive lost fragrance. Essential oils are found in all aromatic plants and give flowers, leaves, seeds, roots and woods their specific smell. These oils are also useful when preparing a pot pourri. This French word meaning "rotten pot" is used to describe an aromatic accessory made from a mixture of perfumed petals, leaves, stems and flower heads, perhaps with added spices and a fixative such as orris root which "fixes" the medley of scents. Pot pourri can be made in one of two ways. The traditional method involves leaving the mixture to rot in a container for several weeks and then placing it in a perforated jar or box so that the scent can escape. Contemporary pot pourris are made by leaving the ingredients to dry in a warm place (though not in direct sunlight) and then placing them in a bowl – you can bring the scents to life again with a few drops of essential oil. To make a pot pourri choose your materials for their scents as well as their colours. The aromatic leaves of lemon verbena (*Aloysia triphylla*) and myrtle (*Myrtus*) can be mixed with scarlet bergamot flowers (*Monarda didyma*), French marigolds (*Tagetes patula*) and heady costmary (*Chrysanthemum balsamita*).

When cut flowers are out of season or in short supply you can force narcissi (*Narcissus tazetta*) and hyacinth (*Hyacinthus*) bulbs indoors; these will exude a heavy, sweet smell. Scented wreaths make a special present or table decoration and are a good way to use herbs from the garden or flowers which are past their best. In the 19th century, heady floral scents were so popular that people grew violets (*Viola odorata*) in lidded glass jars. The glass kept the air around the flowers humid and the lid was lifted to release the potent wafts. Another 19th-century practice was to float the heads of stemless flowers such as wintersweet (*Chimonanthus praecox*) in bowls of water. Not only is this a way of using broken heads, but the idea can be adapted to all sorts of scented flowers and shallow containers. There is a place for scented flowers all over the house. In the kitchen, fresh bunches of planted varieties such as citrus fruit and peppermint-scented geraniums (*Pelargonium*) or dried wreaths and hangings will combat cooking smells.

SUMMER FRAGRANCE

1 *First condition the cut flowers, leaving them in nutrient-enriched water for several hours.*

Take a cylindrical glass container and place it inside a larger glass container of the same shape. Then crumple some medium-gauge chicken or mesh wire into a loose ball and place it inside the smaller, inner container. Fill the inner container with water. Assemble the cut flowers and foliage and the rose-petal pot pourri.

2 *Taking handfuls of scented pot pourri, infill the space in-between the inner and the outer containers: because of the transparency of the glass the dried rose petals will be visible; this makes an interesting feature of the container. You can use any dried plant material which blends with the colour scheme of the*

Flowers
Honeysuckle *(Lonicera)*
Lavender *(Lavandula)*
Sweet pea *(Lathyrus odoratus)*
'Blue Moon' rose *(Rosa 'Blue Moon')*
'Dupontii' rose *(Rosa 'Dupontii')*
'Felicia' rose *(Rosa 'Felicia')*
Mock orange *(Philadelphus)*
Perennial pea *(Lathyrus latifolius)*

Dried flowers
Pot pourri – made from a variety of rose petals

Foliage
Senecio *(Senecio greahi)*
Eucalyptus *(Eucalyptus)*

flower arrangement, for example dessicated petals or leaf, but pot pourri, envigorated with a drop of essential oil, will smell sweetly.

3 *Establish the overall shape of the arrangement with stems of senecio, eucalyptus, mock orange and sprigs of lavender, bunched together to provide greater visual impact. Then add the taller spray 'Dupontii' and 'Felicia' roses.*

4 *Add the sweet peas and the perennial peas, making sure that the arrangement is well-balanced. Use the honeysuckle trails to conceal any mechanics and give a feeling of movement. Fill in any remaining gaps with 'Blue Moon' roses. The finished Summer fragrance arrangement is highly scented and is illustrated on the previous page.*

Containers

Just like the frame of a picture, the container plays an integral part in the overall effect of a flower arrangement. Building up a collection of containers is a must for any flower enthusiast and a good variety will give you maximum scope for creativity. The containers I use come in all shapes, sizes, colours and textures and are made of pottery, china, glass, wood, wicker, stone and metal. I also adapt from more unusual items, such as large fruits and vegetables, to hold flowers. To a certain degree, each individual receptacle dictates the kind of flowers I place in it. For instance, a rustic basket or an old-fashioned watering can will suit bushy, informal displays of country or garden flowers whereas a stream-lined Art Deco vase calls for elegant lilies *(Lilium)* and ivy *(Hedera)* trails.

Not only will the proportions and appearance of a container determine the type of flowers you choose for making an arrangement – a tall receptacle requires long-stemmed blooms and a tiny bowl or a teacup is best suited to small, delicate varieties – but the diameter of the mouth of the vessel is equally important. Narrow-necked vases accommodate slim, smooth stems most easily, while wide-necked containers require a substantial amount of plant material in order to prevent the stems from flopping against the rim in an unsightly manner. So long as your chosen container is not made of glass you should use a crumpled ball of chicken or mesh wire hidden inside it which will support the stems and enable them to be evenly distributed. It is best to use medium- or large-gauge chicken wire to hold the flowers: if the mesh is too small you will have difficulty inserting the stems. You should add the longest stems and the foliage first, then add the shorter stems afterward to fill in any gaps in the arrangement. Once you have finished arranging fill the container with water, making sure that all the stem ends are below the surface; keep the water topped up at all times. An alternative technique which ensures that stems fall evenly in a wide-mouthed vase or bowl is to place the flowers individually into the container at different angles so that their stems intertwine in a criss-cross pattern and so lend each other natural support. If you create a close enough web of interlocking stems, when you want to change the water you should be able to remove the entire bunch and replace it intact. You should cut all the blooms to roughly the same length; first build up the stems around the rim of the container and then add the rest of the flowers to the middle of the receptacle. A third method for achieving a well-balanced display is to arrange the flowers in a tied bunch before placing them into a container (see Techniques, page 175). Once the stems are secured with string simply drop the bunch into a vase, pot or jug: you may then cut the string if you wish.

As a general rule the deeper the container, the longer most cut flowers will last as this allows the stems maximum contact with the water. Tall containers also have the advantage of providing excellent support for plant material while shallow receptacles can pose problems and unless the flowers are cut short and packed in tightly they will not be held in position. However, you can overcome this disadvantage by first placing a florist's spike or "frog" (see Techniques, pages 172-3) in the middle of the bottom of a shallow bowl and then wedging a block of florist's foam onto the spike: this firm, moist base is the starting point for arranging. When using blocks of florist's foam you should have some extra foliage or perhaps pieces of moss or lichen to hand in order to conceal the mechanics. A simple and decorative way to use a shallow container is to fill it with water and float flower heads – perhaps gerberas *(Gerbera)* or anemones *(Anemone)* – and some bobbing candles on the surface. This makes a very attractive table display for a celebration meal.

When choosing your container you must also consider its colour and texture. Most of the containers illustrated in this book look a little aged. I am always drawn toward rusty urns and vases, distressed baskets, tarnished silver, discoloured copper, chipped bran tubs and weathered terra-cotta pots as these worn finishes complement the freshness of cut flowers particularly well. Nowadays all sorts of containers can be bought in a ready-made "aged" condition, or you can experiment with paints and try changing the appearance of plain receptacles using recommended methods of antiquing, marbling, glazing and gilding.

In contrast to a decorative or textured container, a plain glass container hardly competes with the colour of your plant material and for this reason shows off blooms to their full advantage. Quite tightly packed bunches of, for instance, smooth-stemmed daffodils *(Narcissus)* or tulips *(Tulipa)* look particularly striking in a straight-sided glass container. The standard fishbowl shape has the advantage of a relatively narrow neck which supports the flowers and helps them to fall into a natural spiral. I am also fond of Alvar Aalto vases which have a wonderfully fluid feel and wavy sides; they are available in various colours, including a rich, deep blue which harmonizes with blooms of all sorts – cornflowers *(Centaurea)*, brodiaea *(Brodiaea)*, poppies *(Papaver)* and ranunculus *(Ranunculus)* all sit well in these irregularly shaped vessels. From beautiful antique vases to widely available contemporary cylinders, cubes and spheres, glass containers have the unique quality of transparency, so revealing the flower stems. This has both advantages and disadvantages to the flower arranger. Providing you remove all the leaves below the water level, then stems can look attractive underwater. However, if you do not strip away unwanted leaves they quickly turn the water green and slimy. You should wash dirty stems and it is advisable to singe sappy stems such as euphorbias *(Euphorbia)* which ooze an unpleasant milky substance into the water. In order to enhance the appearance of the arrangement and prolong the life of cut flowers, it is necessary to keep both the container and the water inside it clean. Before you begin arranging, wash glass vases or bowls thoroughly with warm water mixed with a small amount of household bleach or even a sprinkling of salt or a good squeeze of lemon – these help to kill bacteria and remove stubborn watermarks. Cut-glass can sometimes be difficult to keep clean; it is best to leave it to soak in warm water mixed with a few drops of vinegar, then rinse and dry. When cleaning fine china you should only use lukewarm, soapy water and never apply detergent as this will make any pattern fade; always rinse with cold water. If you possess an alabaster vase then this may be kept clean by rubbing the surface with a cloth dipped in olive oil. A thin bottle brush is an essential for cleaning narrow-necked vases designed for holding lilies or single specimens. You should change the water regularly in all types of containers, but in glass receptacles this is especially important as murky water really spoils a display. If you use a commercial cut-flower feed to enrich the water with nutrients you must follow the mixing instructions carefully otherwise the water may look cloudy. In areas with "hard" water supplies you may find that the feed makes your water appear chalky – this is because of the relatively high content of lime; one solution is to use bottled spring water. However, if you like the texture of glass but do not find visible stems attractive then there are many opaque alternatives to choose from, for instance, bubbled, frosted, smoked, engraved, coloured, mottled and mother-of-pearl glass. As well as the variety of receptacles designed specifically for holding and displaying flowers, tumblers, bowls, jugs and carafes can all be adapted for arranging purposes.

Glass specimen vases are not always easy to use, as when a top-heavy stem is inserted they easily topple over. However, these containers are currently enjoying a revival and although they were originally developed for tulips *(Tulipa)* they suit all sorts of medium-sized stems, in particular roses *(Rosa)*. I am very fond of so-called lily vases. These tall, elegant vessels can be found in antique shops and good modern replicas are also made. Their slenderness and height restrict the number of stems you can

add, but the overall impression is invariably graceful. Longi lilies *(Lilium longiflorum)* and 'Casablanca' lilies *(Lilium 'Casablanca')* look spectacular in these vases and tumbling stems of Phalaenopsis orchids *(Phalaenopsis)* laden with their white, moth-like heads also look exquisite. In general, tall lily vases are ideal for displaying stems laden with heavy flower heads – they support the length of the stem, so reducing the risk of it snapping. In contrast, smaller 19th-century celery vases, originally designed to hold sticks of celery, are suitable for shorter stems such as droopy 'Parrot' tulips *(Tulipa 'Parrot')*. In addition, all sorts of bulbs look delightful either grown in or transplanted once in bud into glass containers. You can mix soil and peat moss in horizontal layers creating a striped effect which is visible through the glass and the intricate root systems of bulbs lend added interest to the whole arrangement.

The transparent quality of glass allows you to experiment with lining the inside of a glass cylinder, cube or bowl with all sorts of decorative materials such as pot pourri (see pages 44-5) or moss (see pages 28-9). You can also try placing pebbles, marbles, horse chestnuts or miniature fruit or vegetables at the bottom of the receptacle – these help to support weak stems and, submerged in water, they will look shiny and make an original feature of the container. When attempting this kind of decorative effect I advise placing a smaller vessel inside the outer glass container and arranging the flowers in this inner vessel as they will then have the benefit of clean water. In this way the space in-between the inner and outer containers can be kept dry for decorative material such as dried petals and spices or herbs, which should not come into contact with water. This technique of

displaying unusual materials inside a glass vessel can also be adapted to dried flower arrangements. For instance, pine cones, seedheads and dried leaves all complement dried stems. In the kitchen you can experiment with dried pasta shapes and nuts or, if the arrangement is for a bathroom, add shells or coloured sand to liven up a glass container.

Whether it takes the form of a large urn or a simple weathered pot, I enjoy arranging in terra-cotta, for its warm colour contrasts well with the more vivid hues of cut flowers. The term terra-cotta means "fired earth" and covers a wide variety of shades from the pale buff clay generally found in France to the glowing orangey red of most Italian pottery. Unglazed pots and crocks will not hold water and you should always place a waterproof container such as a polystyrene cup, inside them. Avoid placing terra-cotta directly onto a pale cloth as it tends to stain.

While glass containers expose the entire length of cut stems, ceramic containers have the advantage of concealing the twisted, gnarled and unsightly stems of some flowers. The variety of glazes is enormous and ranges from simple monochrome finishes to pots decorated with multi-coloured ethnic patterns. The more patterned and colourful the glaze, the less easy it is to use the container successfully and prevent it from clashing visually with the flowers. Very bright or gaudy containers may steal the eye and kill the impact of blooms altogether, so to reduce the risk of this make a single-colour arrangement which reflects the colour scheme of the container so that the overall effect does not jar.

In general I find that very fine china is impractical for arranging, not only is it fragile but the narrow necks of most china vases are restricting.

Below: The colours of a striped vase are picked out by smoke bush (Cotinus), rudbeckia (Rudbeckia), 'Magi' orchid (Dendrobium 'Magi'), tansy (Tanacetum), red hot pokers (Kniphofia), bupleurum (Bupleurum), viburnum berries (Viburnum), gerberas (Gerbera), spiky amaranthus (Amaranthus hypochondriacus) and yellow arums (Zantedeschia).

Right. A varied selection of pottery, unglazed terracotta and fired ceramic containers. Below: Golden rod (Solidago), fennel (Foeniculum), snowberry (Symphoricarpos albus), privet (Ligustrum), sunflowers (Helianthus), delphiniums (Delphinium), hanging amaranthus (Amaranthus caudatus) and ivy (Hedera) complement a blue ceramic vase.

However, I do like to use blue and white patterned china, particularly Dutch flower bricks which are now reproduced with attractive glazes. The brick features a number of holes, allowing stems to be inserted and they are ideal for dried flower arrangements. I also have a penchant for antique spongeware jugs which have wide mouths, allowing for plenty of plant material. If you have a shortage of pottery containers you can always adapt kitchen vessels such as mustard pots and jugs or pitchers.

Large terra-cotta or stone urns are fun to use when arranging for a special occasion. Do not be put off by the size of the urn as you can always infill the bottom with crumpled chicken or mesh wire. Very often urns can be heavy and once filled with water they can be difficult to move. For this reason you should arrange once the container is in situ. If this isn't possible you can place a smaller inner vessel inside the urn for the stems to drink from; wedge the inner container firmly inside using crumpled balls of newpaper. Even though urns are weighty and cumbersome they never fail to create a grand impression and they are so stable that there is little risk of the arrangement toppling over. You should line the vessel with a large plastic bag or sheet to protect the inside from scratches caused by hard stem ends or chicken wire. A removable lining will also speed up the cleaning-up process when the arrangement is dismantled.

Just as the warm, earthy hues of pottery complement the vivacious colours of many cut blooms and the cool green of foliage, so the natural browns of wooden containers and baskets work in the same way. Baskets

Right. All sorts of wooden containers can be used. The giant hogweed
(Heracleum mantegazzianum) is highly toxic so only use this dried.
Below: I covered an old metal bin with birch (Betula) twigs, made flexible by soaking them
in water. The fluffy cotton (Gossypium) contrasts well with the the texture of the twigs.

and wooden receptacles are as permeable as unglazed pottery and similarly, they must be made watertight before flowers can be arranged in them. The versatility of wood offers the flower arranger all kinds of inspiring possibilities as so many varieties are available and it is a material which can be inexpensively garnered from a garden or hedgerow (you can also strip away the outer bark from pieces of wood for a clean, smooth texture). Not only can you use containers such as gardening trugs, old barrels and ethnic baskets which come in a host of shapes, sizes, weaves and colours, but you can also adapt a base from unusual pieces of tree trunk, bark or driftwood, perhaps picked up on a country or seaside walk. The great advantage of arranging in baskets is that they are often made with handles and so are easily transportable, making them ideal containers for holding gift arrangements.

Other interesting adaptations are not difficult to make. For instance, try covering an ordinary cylindrical or straight-sided container with double-sided tape; then take twigs, sticks or pieces of bamboo cut to even lengths and attach them in a vertical "fencing" pattern all around the container. In the same way you can use elongated vegetables such as green beans *(Phaseolus vulgaris)*, cinnamon sticks, *(Cinnamomum zeylanicum)*, rhubarb *(Rheum rhaponticum)*, celery *(Apium graveolens)*, leeks *(Allium ampeloprasum porrum)* and asparagus *(Asparagus officinalis)* and place them horizontally or vertically around a receptacle. Another idea is to arrange thick twigs or small branches of a similar size and length at right angles to each other so that they form a square shape; bind the construction together with string and line it before use. When you have finished arranging – perhaps a planted bulb display – moss or lichen will fill any

Left: Some ideas for adapting plant material to make "natural" containers.
Below: Sunflower (Helianthus) seedheads, with the petals removed, can be attached using double-sided adhesive tape and glue to transform an ordinary fishbowl. Contorted willow (Salix matsudana 'Contorta'), globe artichokes (Cynara scolymus), Bells of Ireland (Moluccella), rudbeckia (Rudbeckia) and fennel (Foeniculum) blend well together.

gaps and conceal visible patches of lining. You can also transform plain containers by sticking jute or hessian sacking, coils of thick rope, string, ribbon or raffia around them.

Certain varieties of fruit and vegetables can be adapted to make original containers which are particularly effective as table arrangements, as the raw materials used link the edible theme of the display to food. However, because all plant material gives off ethylene gas as it matures, these organic containers unfortunately do not last long and hence they are only suitable for one-off special occasions as they will only look their best for a day or two.

I find large fruit and vegetables easiest to work with. First remove the fleshy insides. Next place a plastic lining inside the skin and fill the void with florist's foam – this is the base for your arrangement. Traditionally, the vegetable most commonly used for decorative purposes is the pumpkin *(Cucurbita maxima)*, although all the squash family, in particular gourds *(Cucurbita)*, make good, firm bases. Hollowed-out melons *(Cucumis melo)*, coconuts *(Cocos nucifera)* and globe artichokes *(Cynara scolymus)* offer further possibilities. For small-scale arrangements peppers *(Capsicum)* or courgettes *(Cucurbita pepo)* can be adapted for a dinner-table arrangement.

To create a different style of "natural" container I often cover plain receptacles with double-sided tape and attach leaves such as Galax *(Galax)* or glossy Laurel *(Laurelia)* all around the exterior. In fact, any large, flat and shiny variety of leaf fulfills the same function. Alternatively, you can remove the prime inner leaves of cabbages *(Brassica oleracea capitata alba)* and wrap them around the outside of a bowl, securing them with string, raffia or even plaited fronds of bear grass *(Dasylirion)*. The mauve leaves of ornamental cabbage or the crinkly leaves of Savoy cabbage are particularly decorative. Lettuce *(Lactua sativa)* or the leaves of endives or chicory *(Cichorium endiva)* can be used in the same way to create an attractive "leaf bowl". All sorts of miniature fruit and vegetables, nuts or even flat-headed flowers such as sunflowers *(Helianthus)* will also adhere to double-sided tape, so the possibilities for decorating containers are endless!

I find that very shiny metal containers tend to draw the eye away from flowers on display and so I invariably prefer the look of worn, beaten or weathered metal. For example, a loose mass of country or garden flowers in a simple tin or galvanized bucket is hard to better and all sorts of utilitarian household receptacles such as tin or copper pans or skillets and even old bird cages

and wire egg baskets make attractive containers for both fresh and dried arrangements. Old silver wine coolers or ice buckets, pewter jugs or tankards, rusty Victorian urns and multi-tiered *épergnes* – originally used for cascading displays of fruit and flowers – are some of my favourite metal containers. The main advantage of metal is that it is cold and so keeps flowers cool. However, even a watertight metal vessel should be lined as its surface will corrode if it comes into contact with moisture.

The colour and texture of your chosen metal receptacle will naturally influence your choice of flowers: heavy cast iron goes well with bright primary reds, yellows and blues; silver and pewter blend happily with delicate blues, mauves, purples and pinks and warm, autumnal shades of orange, russet and brown combine happily with copper and bronze surfaces. The vivid green and blue shades of verdigris are currently in vogue and this metal effect contrasts beautifully with blue and white flowers and dark green foliage.

Perhaps one of the most effective ways of using a metal base is in the form of a candlestick – whether it is a large pedestal such as the one illustrated in the Easter arrangement (see page 126) or a more refined silver candelabra used in the silver wedding anniversary arrangement (see page 154). Candles never fail to draw the eye and create a special ambience. In order to arrange successfully around a metal candleholder you should acquire candle cups (see Techniques, pages 172–3) which fit snugly into candlesticks and simultaneously support a block of florist's foam. If you wish to decorate a very large candelabra simply tape blocks florist's foam tightly around the bottom of the candle using water-resistant florist's tape. In either case you soon have a ready-made base and can start arranging your flowers and foliage by simply inserting the stems.

Above: A modern metal conservatory stand suitable for a formal celebration. First wire fresh moss evenly around the spiralled frame so that no metal remains visible. Then cover the moss with grouped sprigs of skimmia (Skimmia), viburnum (Viburnum) and hydrangea heads (Hydrangea macrophylla). Wire in clusters of pine cones, dried mushrooms, gourds (Cucurbita), berries and bundles of small twigs (see Techniques, pages 176–7). Place a pot in the top of the stand and arrange stems of ornamental peppers (Capsicum frutescens), clove-coloured amaranthus (Amaranthus) and berried foliage in wet florist's foam.
Left: A dense spray of snapdragons (Antirrhinum) and some eucalyptus (Eucalyptus) leaves loosely arranged in a 19th-century French painted tin receptacle.
Right: An assortment of metal containers which can be adapted for holding flowers and will keep stems cool.

Colour
Themes

Colours are defined according to the colour spectrum. Yellow, red and blue are the three so-called primaries and combine to produce the secondary colours of orange, green and purple. A simple and also an invariably successful approach to colour themes is to work with flowers of one colour only and use various shades of your chosen single colour in order to give the display texture.

Your choice of colours will be dictated by the time of year. One of the joys of flower arranging is that as the seasons change so the hues of flowers alter, and your choices of plant material will be influenced by seasonal availability. In the northern hemisphere we associate fresh yellows and blues with spring and an abundance of hues from soft pastels to hot primary colours with summer. By autumn or fall the predominant shades are reds, oranges and yellows, while in the winter we rely on all sorts of foliage, fruits and nuts for colour. However, the international flower market is so advanced today that imported flowers break the old seasonal boundaries and many "all-year-around" flowers such as chrysanthemums *(Chrysanthemum)* and carnations *(Dianthus)*, including their many spray varieties, are always available in all kinds of tints.

I find two particular colours are especially versatile. First, white (although it isn't strictly a colour) which will provide contrast and lighten the overall effect of other massed blooms. Because of its neutrality white can be mixed with any plant material and will bring a dark arrangement to life. Second, green which both harmonizes with and vitalizes other hues and can be mixed successfully with all colours of the spectrum.

Colours are commonly described in terms of temperature; blues and greens are perceived as "cool", while reds, oranges and yellows are referred to as "hot". Because cool colours appear to recede they are especially suitable in arrangements placed in a light setting and seen from close-to. By contrast, a glowing yellow arrangement or a white display which reflects light are well suited to a darker setting and will be noticed when viewed from a distance. Context is all-important – you should always take into account the backdrop for your arrangement and make sure that your chosen flowers complement the colour schemes of any surrounding walls, furnishings, drapes and table setting. Containers are equally relevant, and will be seen as an integral part of the overall arrangement. You can choose the flowers to suit the colour of the container, or vice versa, or you can play safe and use plain terra-cotta and earthenware containers which complement almost all varieties of plant material.

Whether you prefer the warm hues of reds and yellows, the coolness of blues and greens or the purity of whites and creams, colour is both a delightful and a constantly challenging aspect of flower arranging. When it comes to creating mixed arrangements you should allow your own subjectivity to influence you. Everyone has different ideas of which colours clash, although Nature seems to ignore the very idea of incongruous colours. All sorts of duo-tone flowers can give hints of how to mix colours well. For example, if you look closely at a bird of paradise *(Strelitzia reginae)* you will see that bright orange and purple blend happily together – so why not build a whole arrangement on the theme?

The red spectrum offers flower arrangers endless scope and an enormous variety of blooms encompassing soft pinks, bright scarlets and vermilions, vibrant oranges and magentas, warm russets and rich burgundies. Among its host of associations red conveys good will, warmth and passion. Throughout the year this colour is a universal favourite and its popularity reaches a peak during the build-up to Saint Valentine's Day. The huge demand for red roses at this time of year is answered by international commercial growers who produce quantities of prime stems such as the appropriately named 'Only Love' roses (*Rosa* 'Only Love') and 'Idole' roses (*Rosa* 'Idole'). At the international Dutch flower auctions (see pages 11–15) eager bidders force the prices of these archetypal tokens of love to a premium during the days leading up to February 14.

Red is a so-called "advancing" colour because it draws the eye so effectively. For this reason it has always been a popular choice for gift flowers on all sorts of occasions, from romantic offerings to farewell tributes. The poppy (*Papaver*), whose brilliant red heads sprang up on the battlefields of World War I, is a symbolic reminder of human life for Europeans. However, just as a red rose need not be interpreted simply as a message of passion, so poppies are much more than sobering symbols of war or "consolation" flowers. Indeed, their papery scarlet petals are bright and cheerful, and thanks to new European legislation restricting intensive agricultural practices, we should soon see more fields carpeted with wild poppies. The wild variety should be picked while still in bud and all poppy stems should be sealed with a flame in order to prevent them oozing and make the flowers last (see Techniques, page 174).

Red flowers are particularly popular during the Christmas period. The upright variety of amaranthus (*Amaranthus hypochondriacus*) comes in a deep red, as does the lovely hanging variety, romantically known as love-lies-bleeding (*Amaranthus caudatus*), and both types add a rich texture to Christmas arrangements. Amaranthus dries well and retains its colouring; fresh or dry it is complemented by dark green foliage such as spruce (*Picea*), camellia (*Camellia japonica*) or mahonia (*Mahonia*). Some of my other favourite Christmas flowers are big black-eyed 'Beauty' gerberas (*Gerbera* 'Beauty'), the spectacular heads of amaryllis (*Hippeastrum*) and the smaller "pygmy" amaryllis variety. The hollow stems of the amaryllis have to support heavy flowering "trumpets"; you should insert a thin garden cane into the stem to prevent the flower head from drooping or breaking off.

Also, you can fill the hollow stems with water and plug them with a ball of cotton wool, this will help increase the life of the blooms and keep them looking fresh (see Techniques, page 174). The poinsettia (*Euphorbia pulcherrima*) is universally associated with Christmas, and, attractive as it is, the flower is temperamental and sensitive to drafts. If you cut poinsettias you should seal them by exposing the stem ends to a flame (see Techniques, page 174). All sorts of red berries, fruits and seed pods come into

Red

Right: To make a red theme arrangement I found a large old iron bran tub to hold a quantity of flowers. Then I placed crumpled chicken or mesh wire inside the tub to provide support for the stems: without this they would not remain in the required position. The display includes a rich variety of colour co-ordinated red and orange blooms grouped into bunches to give visual impact. The scattered leaves are dried and glycerined laurel (Laurus).

season during the winter months in Europe and North America. Their contrasting shapes and textures make delightful Christmas decorations and they have the added advantage of lasting well. For example, the leafless variety of holly (*Ilex verticillata*) with its woody, berry-laden stems, bright red cotoneaster (*Cotoneaster*), hawthorn (*Crataegus*), skimmia (*Skimmia japonica*) and yew (*Taxus baccata*) are all fun to use, while pink snowberries (*Symphoricarpos*), orange Chinese lanterns (*Physalis*) and miniature orange and red ornamental peppers (*Capsicum frutescens*) offer other alternatives.

Roses are perhaps the flowers most commonly associated with the colour red. Of all the hundreds of varieties of red roses, one of my favourites is the almost black 'Baccarolla' rose (*Rosa* 'Baccarolla'), which is illustrated in the Edible Valentine arrangement on page 160. Its unusually dark colouring and velvety texture make it more expensive than other roses, but 'Baccarolla' stems mixed with cream-coloured 'Champagne' roses (*Rosa* 'Champagne') make a stunning display. Because red is a strong colour which arrests the eye, it is generally easier to combine it with more restrained shades such as whites and creams, or else you can break up the impact of red blooms with foliage. If you wish to play down a vibrant red you can use a dark green foliage such as wood spurge (*Euphorbia amygdaloides*), rue (*Ruta graveolens*), hellebore (*Helleborus*) – which lasts well once cut – or the lovely catkin tassels of the male silk tassel bush (*Garrya elliptica*). Conversely, more muted shades of red can be livened up with lighter or acid green foliage such as the long-lasting elaeagnus (*Elaeagnus pungens*), moluccella or bells of Ireland (*Moluccella laevis*), spindle (*Euonymus japonica*) or spirea (*Spirea japonica*).

One of my favourite red flowers is the 'Mona Lisa' anemone (*Anemone* 'Mona Lisa'), and its deep red hue contrasts beautifully with a lush and shiny green leaf such as laurel (*Laurelia*). You can try making a laurel-covered vase, as illustrated on page 4, and fill it with red anemones. All you have to do is take a cylindrical container such as a glass and cover it with leaves using double-sided adhesive tape, then fill the container with water and add some red anemones. I am also fond of gerberas (*Gerbera*) which come in all sorts of reds, pinks and oranges. Because of their large, flat heads these flowers are particularly suitable for floating in a shallow bowl of water. This simple procedure makes an attractive table arrangement; just cut off the stems and float the gerbera heads on the surface of the water.

The fieriness of orange makes it a challenging colour to arrange with, but with a little daring the results can be stunning. I like to use orange alone, perhaps in a simple bunch of ranunculus (*Ranunculus*) or dahlias (*Dahlia*), or mixed with red, mauve, peach or blue. Although I rarely combine orange and yellow flowers, fruits and vegetables such as gourds look effective together, particularly if mixed with foliage and browns and russets, as in the Halloween or Thanksgiving arrangement on pages 134–5. Some of my favourite orange flowers are South African Leucospermum (*Leucospermum nutans*), which are also called nodding pin cushions, a

Fiery reds

1 Glory lily *(Gloriosa superba)*
2 Lily *(Lilium)*
3 Ginger heliconia *(Heliconia)*
4 Carnation *(Dianthus)*
5 Bouvardia *(Bouvardia)*
6 Statice *(Limonium)*
7 Snowberry *(Symphoricarpos)*
8 Pineapple *(Ananas comosus)*
9 'Dutch Beauty' rose *(Rosa* 'Dutch Beauty')
10 'Diadeen' rose *(Rosa* 'Diadeen')
11 Lily *(Amaryllis belladonna)*
12 Cock's comb *(Celosia argentea)*
13 Chrysanthemum *(Chrysanthemum)*
14 Lily *(Lilium longiflorum)*
15 'Jacaranda' rose *(Rosa* 'Jacaranda')
16 Astilbe *(Astilbe simplicifolia)*
17 Anemone *(Anemone)*
18 Delphinium *(Delphinium)*
19 Snapdragon *(Antirrhinum)*
20 Gladiolus *(Gladiolus)*
21 Ice-plant *(Sedum spectabile)*
22 'James Storei' orchid *(Dendrobium)*
23 Heliconia *(Heliconia)*
24 'Baccarolla' rose *(Rosa* 'Baccarolla')
25 Gerbera *(Gerbera)*
26 Amaranthus *(Amaranthus)*
27 Hydrangea *(Hydrangea)*
28 'Nikita' rose *(Rosa* 'Nikita')
29 Globe amaranth *(Gomphrena)*
30 Bouvardia *(Bouvardia)*
31 'Alpha' phlox *(Phlox* 'Alpha')
32 Chrysanthemum *(Chrysanthemum)*
33 Lily *(Lilium)*
34 Cock's comb *(Celosia argentea)*
35 Amaryllis *(Hippeastrum)*
36 Carnation *(Dianthus)*
37 Tulip *(Tulipa)*
38 'First Red' rose *(Rosa* 'First Red')
39 Guernsey lily *(Nerine sarniensis)*
40 Ginger heliconia *(Heliconia)*
41 Montbretia *(Crocosmia)*
42 Silk weed *(Asclepias)*
43 Carnation *(Dianthus)*
44 Cock's comb *(Celosia argentea)*
45 Alstroemeria *(Alstroemeria)*
46 Chrysanthemum *(Chrysanthemum)*
47 Leucospermum *(Leucospermum)*
48 Dahlia *(Dahlia)*
49 Carnation *(Dianthus)*
50 Chrysanthemum *(Chrysanthemum)*
51 Painter's palette *(Anthurium)*
52 Gerbera *(Gerbera)*
53 'Red Ace' rose *(Rosa* 'Red Ace')
54 'Vicky Brown' rose *(Rosa* 'Vicky Brown')
55 Achillea *(Achillea)*
56 Guelder rose *(Viburnum opulus)*
57 Hypericum *(Hypericum)*
58 Freesia *(Freesia)*
59 Waratah *(Telopea speciosissima)*

Left: On a pink theme, a basketful of ixea (Ixea), ranunculus (Ranunculus), lily-of-the-valley (Convallaria majalis), 'Angelique' tulips (Tulipa 'Angelique'), ornamental pineapples (Ananas comosus) and blossom.
Right: A warm orange arrangement of marigolds (Calendula), ranunculus (Ranunculus), silk weed (Asclepias) and lady's mantle (Alchemilla mollis).
Below: A strong-hued bouquet balancing on its own stems (see Techniques, page 175). Includes masterwort (Astrantia), foxgloves (Digitalis), 'Star Gazer' lilies (Lilium speciosum 'Star Gazer'), peonies (Paeonia), 'Jacaranda' roses (Rosa 'Jacaranda'), thistles (Eryngium alpinium) and also sweet peas (Lathyrus odoratus).
Overleaf: A display showing heliconia (Heliconia), cock's comb (Celosia argentea) and bright-green silkweed (Asclepias physocarpa) seed pods.

name that accurately describes their rounded, spiky heads; the tall, straight stems of red hot pokers *(Kniphofia)* and the wispy stems of montbretia *(Crocosmia)*. Although some people regard orange as an unsubtle colour which is difficult to blend with domestic interiors, it is a particularly suitable choice for offices as its cheerfulness contrasts well with the neutral tones of many work environments. You can set off bright orange with purple-coloured foliage such as cotinus, also known as smoke bush *(Cotinus)*, sweet gum *(Liquidambar styraciflua)*, copper beech *(Fagus sylvatica purpurea)* and berberis *(Berberis thunbergii atropurpurea)*. The arrangement of marigolds *(Calendula officinalis)* and asclepias *(Ascelpias)* on page 75 is one of my favourite monochromatic combinations and I chose a dark vase to contrast with the orange petals and tone down the overall effect. The most vibrant blooms are best played down with a sober colour, otherwise the effect is overpowering and uneasy on the eye. Too many vivid petals of different hues used in combination vie for attention and the final result is that the colours compete and often clash instead of harmonizing.

Pink, which is perceived as a particularly feminine colour, is a common favourite among brides for wedding bouquets and decoration and it is often chosen to celebrate the birth of a newborn baby girl. Pinks range from the lightest-hued blooms such as 'Little Silver' roses *(Rosa 'Little Silver')*, 'Upstar' tulips *(Tulipa 'Upstar')*, 'Le Reve' lilies *(Lilium 'Le Reve')* and delicate sweet peas *(Lathyrus odoratus)* to the hotter shades of celosias or cock's comb *(Celosia argentea)*, heliconias *(Heliconia)*, stocks *(Matthiola)*, red valerian *(Centranthus ruber)* and 'Jacaranda' roses *(Rosa 'Jacaranda')*. In the spring I love to use pink 'Angelique' tulips *(Tulipa 'Angelique')* mixed with soft blues and in the summer I arrange peonies *(Paeonia)* and foxgloves *(Digitalis)* with chervil *(Anthriscus)* and lime-green lady's mantle *(Alchemilla mollis)* or bushy guelder rose *(Viburnum opulus)*.

Between pink and yellow is an array of colours from peach to apricot. The most widely available varieties in these shades are chrysanthemums *(Chrysanthemum)*, carnations *(Dianthus)* and gladioli *(Gladiolus)* – all of which are now bred in all sorts of colours. Also common are alstroemerias *(Alstroemeria)*, gerberas *(Gerbera)*, iceland poppies *(Papaver nudicaule)* and the lovely double hollyhock *(Alcea rosea)* – although unfortunately its beauty is short-lived as the flowers do not last well. Among my favourite peach-coloured flowers are tawny-hued ranunculus *(Ranunculus)* which hold their attraction well as their fading petals turn light and fluffy; peach amaryllis *(Hippeastrum)* which look stunning arranged in a tall sturdy vase with tortured willow *(Salix matsudana 'Tortuosa')* or with their stems cut short in a shallow container, and beautiful 'Osiana' roses *(Rosa 'Osiana')*. Mauves and blues mix well with peach, orange and rust-coloured flowers.

The versatility of red and its myriad shades from pastel peaches and pinks to rich ruby means that it can provide an appropriate colour theme for any kind of flower arrangement and any sort of special occasion, whether it is a grand bridal bouquet of 'Prominence' lilies *(Lilium 'Prominence')*, a scented posy of sweet Williams *(Dianthus barbatus)* for a Mother's Day gift or a bold birthday display of tropical heliconias *(Heliconia)* or birds of paradise *(Strelitzia reginae)*. The selection of red, pink and orange flowers I use during the year is illustrated on pages 72-3.

Yellow is a primary colour which appears to "advance" because of its high level of luminosity. It is immensely popular, for its cheeriness, and it is the hue of the most popular flower in Britain – the daffodil *(Narcissus)*. As yellows are naturally either light or bright in tone, I often use them monochromatically – in other words mixed with other shades of yellow – or else I blend them with the more neutral shades of white or cream. However, blues also blend very successfully with yellows, and although I like to arrange daffodils and narcissi alone, these blooms also combine well with blue hyacinths *(Hyacinthus)* or the delightful miniature stems of grape hyacinths *(Muscari)*. Bulbs such as these, as well as crocuses *(Crocus)*, cyclamen *(Cyclamen)* and tulips *(Tulipa)*, can be forced when many fresh flowers are out of season and so hard to come by. If you plant your own bulbs you should fill a bowl or a terra-cotta pot with an equal amount of soil, peat moss and sand and position the bulbs so that their shoots or "noses" are just beneath the surface. Then leave them in a cool, dark place for at least a month and they will flower into an attractive, informal arrangement which will last for several weeks and scent a room beautifully.

I think that daffodils look their best either grown from bulbs in this way, or as cut blooms bunched together on their own in a plain vase. You can make a simple arrangement of daffodils in no time at all by letting them fall evenly in a glass fishbowl or in a terra-cotta pot, the latter will complement the yellow heads well, but you will have to insert a waterproof container inside the porous terra-cotta. Because of their front-facing, trumpet-shaped heads and their straight stems, daffodils are difficult to mix with other flowers. However, so many different types are available that daffodils offer plenty of variety for a yellow-theme display.

The "advancing" quality of yellow means that it stands out in dimly lit areas and works particularly well inside churches or in rooms with dark walls or low lighting. If you are making a large pedestal arrangement which has to be seen from a distance, a duo-tone arrangement of long-stemmed cream delphiniums *(Delphinium)* and stocks *(Matthiola)* with yellow snapdragons *(Antirrhinum majus)* and some larger heads of 'Urk' lilies *(Lilium 'Urk')* or perhaps 'Yellow Spider' chrysanthemums *(Chrysanthemum 'Yellow Spider')* will make a strong visual impact. The freshness of yellow and white make a good combination.

For a clean, modern look try arranging yellow arum lilies *(Zantedeschia)*, gerberas *(Gerbera)* or the smaller varieties known as germinis

in a plain container which may have an assymetrical shape. Some flowers have a spattering of black which makes them all the more eye-catching and plays down the effect of all-over yellow – consider 'Black-eyed' and 'Poker' gerberas and the similarly speckled 'Florence' lily. There are other predominantly yellow varieties which have a blush of orange or red, such as 'Golden Shower' orchids *(Cymbidium 'Golden Shower')* and 'Cooksbridge' orchids *(Cymbidium 'Cooksbridge')* and the

Yellow

Right: This "vegetative" style of arranging is popular in Europe. I put wet florist's foam in a bark-covered window box and added all sorts of yellow stems, including 'Golden Ducat' daffodils (Narcissus 'Golden Ducat'), 'Widow' irises (Iris 'Widow'), 'Quadricolor' lachenalia (Lachenalia 'Quadricolor') and the flowers and leaf of achillea (Achillea). Strands of bear grass (Dasylirion) help to create the impression of growing plant material.

attractive striped 'Flaming Parrot' tulips *(Tulipa 'Flaming Parrot')* with their lovely feathery petals. There are all sorts of attractive yellow tulips, including the smooth 'Yokohama' or 'Apeldoorn' varieties and the frilly-topped 'Yellow Fancy Thrill'. Tulips live longer in water than they do inserted into a block of florist's foam. If you are concerned to support the stems and prevent them from bending or drooping, use a ball of chicken wire, so long as the container is not transparent. This will allow the flowers to drink easily. Interestingly, tulips continue to grow after they have been cut and

arranged – for this reason the stems may end up several inches or centimetres taller than other varieties if mixed together in an arrangement. You should bear this in mind when arranging as after a few days the elongated stems may break the proportions of your display.

Yellow is a very popular colour for weddings, and there are all sorts of possibilities to choose from. Roses *(Rosa)* such as 'Baroque', 'Cocktail', 'Golden Times' or 'Aalsmeer Gold' can be worked into a bridal bouquet or made into individual buttonholes and corsages with a sprig of foliage. I particularly like to combine 'Bahama' roses with yellow freesias *(Freesia)*, pale 'Porcelain' roses and variegated ivy *(Hedera)* which gives a flowing outline. You can also add trailing honeysuckle *(Lonicera)* to enhance the feeling of movement. Not only will this lend a wonderful smell, but in the "language of flowers" it has appropriate associations with love and constancy.

You can also use large-headed 'Yellow Ribbon' lilies *(Lilium 'Yellow Ribbon')* mixed with fine sprays of solidaster *(Solidaster)* as the basic ingredients of a wedding bouquet. Other yellow lilies which add a special touch to formal arrangements for any kind of special occasion, be it a wedding, an official function or a party, include foxtail lilies *(Eremurus spectabilis)* and 'Regalia' lilies *(Lilium 'Regalia')* which can be mixed together and will last well; foxtail lilies last for up to 18 days if you strip the lower flowers off the stems once they have bloomed. These two varieties make a good combination as the sweeter scent of the 'Regalia' lilies overrides the slightly less pleasant pungent aroma of the foxtails. In order to keep the latter free from odour you should arrange them in water enriched with a suitable commercial cut-flower feed and remember to change the water in the container regularly.

The large heads of crown imperials *(Fritillaria imperialis)* are equally striking and can either be part of a large display or else stand on their own because they are so conspicuous. Sadly they have a short season, and although some people find their musty smell a little off-putting – you can overcome this problem by putting the stems in clean water daily – their radiant petals, curvy stems and big heads make them a firm favourite of mine. As with tulips, the stems tend to be sinuous as the heads move naturally toward the light, but this makes them all the more interesting when massed together in a container (see pages 28–9). There is a touching Biblical story connected to these flowers: when Jesus was taken from the Garden of Gethsemane to his crucifixion, the crown imperial drooped

Glowing yellows

1 African corn lily *(Ixia* 'Spotlight')
2 'Minor' daffodil *(Narcissus* 'Minor')
3 Daffodil *(Narcissus odorus)*
4 'Cragford' daffodil *(Narcissus* 'Cragford')
5 'Cheerfulness' daffodil *(Narcissus* 'Cheerfulness')
6 'Primo' daffodil *(Narcissus* 'Primo')
7 'Baroque' rose *(Rosa* 'Baroque')
8 'Cocktail' rose *(Rosa* 'Cocktail')
9 'Carte d'Or' rose *(Rosa* 'Carte d'Or')
10 'Bellona' freesia *(Freesia* 'Bellona')
11 'Pallas' carnation *(Dianthus* 'Pallas')
12 'Evergold' rose *(Rosa* 'Evergold')
13 'Yokohama' tulip *(Tulipa* 'Yokohama')
14 Alstroemeria *(Alstroemeria)*
15 Solidaster *(Solidago* 'Praecox')
16 'Yellow Fancy Thrill' tulip *(Tulipa* 'Yellow Fancy Thrill')
17 Poppy *(Papaver nudicaule)*
18 Waxflower *(Stephanotis)*
19 'Cooksbridge' orchid *(Cymbidium* 'Cooksbridge')
20 Spurge *(Euphorbia fulgens)*
21 Golden rod *(Solidago)*
22 Spurge *(Euphorbia myrsinites)*
23 Marigold *(Calendula officinalis)*
24 Arum lily *(Zantedeschia)*
25 'Golden Shower' orchid *(Cymbidium* 'Golden Shower')
26 'Grace' freesia *(Freesia* 'Grace')
27 Feverfew *(Chrysanthemum parthenium)*
28 Polyanthus *(Primula polyanthus)*
29 'Golden Ducat' daffodil *(Narcissus* 'Golden Ducat')
30 'Serena' rose *(Rosa* 'Serena')
31 Mimosa *(Acacia dealbata)*
32 Broom *(Genista)*
33 'Urk' lily *(Lilium* 'Urk')
34 Chrysanthemum *(Chrysanthemum)*
35 'Apeldoorn' tulip *(Tulipa* 'Apeldoorn')
36 'Flaming Parrot' tulip *(Tulipa* 'Flaming Parrot')
37 Foxtail lily *(Eremurus spectabilis)*
38 Stock *(Matthiola)*
39 Fennel *(Foeniculum vulgare)*
40 Snapdragon *(Antirrhinum majus)*
41 Achillea *(Achillea)*
42 Forsythia *(Forsythia spectabilis)*
43 Mimosa *(Acacia dealbata)*
44 Heliconia *(Heliconia)*
45 Gerbera *(Gerbera)*
46 Kangeroo paw *(Anigozanthos)*
47 Chrysanthemum *(Chrysanthemum)*
48 Hyacinth *(Hyacinthus)*
49 'Poker' germini *(Gerbera* 'Poker')
50 'Princess' tulip *(Tulipa* 'Princess')
51 Buttercup *(Ranunculus asiaticus)*
52 Primrose *(Primula vulgaris)*

its head in remorse and tears filled its petals. These lovely yellow blooms shed drops of moisture whether they are planted in the ground out doors or freshly cut, and their deep cups continue to hold water long after they have been arranged indoors.

The sunflower *(Helianthus)* is enjoying a revival today. These are wonderful, bold flowers which look just as good growing in a pot – although their long stems need staking to help support the heavy heads – as they do freshly cut. The huge, daisy-like flowers can be removed from the stem and fixed with double-sided adhesive tape to cover a large, rounded container (see page 63). Or you can mix sunflower stems with similar-looking coneflowers *(Rudbeckia)* and red hot pokers *(Kniphofia)*. The sunflower's glowing petals and large dark "eye" provide a useful hint that bright yellows blend well with deeper shades of brown. All sorts of reeds have duller tones which combine harmoniously with yellow blooms, in particular the brown hues of bull-rushes *(Typha latifolia)*. Take care to buy these before the cylindrical seedheads have split as they look messy once the white seeds begin to break away; there are a few commercial mister sprays available which prevent reeds and grasses from spilling their seeds. Both bullrushes and sunflowers dry well, as does mimosa *(Mimosa)*, which also retains its sweet fragrance, and the tight heads of tansies *(Tanacetum vulgare)*. Achillea, or yarrow, *(Achillea)* is another attractive flower, either fresh – the umbrella-shaped heads blend well with irises (see page 113) – or dried. Bright yellow achillea makes a good supplement to a dried display or as the main decorative ingredient of a topiary tree. To make this, fix a branch or a thick twig into a terra-cotta or earthenware pot using plaster of Paris, quick-drying cement or dry-hard florist's clay and attach a round foam ball to the top of the "trunk" before wiring dried achillea into the foam. Some fresh or dried fruits and vegetables – for instance, mushrooms

(Agaricus bisporus), gourds *(Cucurbita)* and pomegranates *(Punica granatum)* – can add an ornamental flourish to plant material. If you wish to dry mushrooms place them on a tray in an airing cupboard or over a radiator. You can wire fresh pomegranates into an arrangement or else scoop out their fleshy interiors and stuff them with newspaper to dry them out. They can then be varnished to enhance their colourful skins. Gourds, which have green, striped or yellow skins also benefit from a coat of varnish. The yellow varieties are fun to use in Halloween or Thanksgiving wreaths, edible table arrangements or Christmas garlands.

As with all other colours, when it comes to mixing yellow with other hues subjectivity comes to the fore and there are no rights or wrongs. Personally I like to mix dark blues or purples with strong golden shades – the petals of irises *(Iris)* do this naturally. For a more restrained look I combine paler lemons with white, cream and a complementary foliage. I tend to avoid mixing very warm yellows with orange, but this combination can work well with very dark, glossy leaves such as camellia *(Camellia)*, laurel *(Laurelia)* and gardenia *(Gardenia)*. The glow of yellow contrasts best with deep green leaves. Some types of yellowy foliage, such as variegated elaeagnus *(Elaeagnus pungens)* or elder *(Sambucus)*, will deaden the impact of flowers of the same colour, so use plenty of dark leaf to provide the necessary contrast. Many of my favourite yellow flowers are illustrated on pages 80–1.

Above: A tumbler disguised with galax (Galax) leaves, filled with pale miniature flowers.
Left: White grape hyacinths (Muscari), hellebores (Helleborus), tuberoses (Polianthes) and narcissi (Narcissus) tied in a bunch with galax leaves and bear grass (Dasylirion).
Right: A terra-cotta pot, containing wet florist's foam, decorated with a candle and blooms.
Overleaf: Ideas for embellishing containers using a variety of small fruits and vegetables.

Green is a secondary colour produced by the fusing of varying degrees of blue and yellow. In the temperate zones of the world it is the predominant colour of the landscape and is soothing to the eye. With its generally tranquil character, green has a weaker visual impact than most other hues and, together with the fact that it is the colour attributed to practically all types of foliage, it is an ideal background or infill shade for flower arrangers. From the dark, evergreen leaves of holly (*Ilex*), spruce (*Picea*), pine (*Pinus*) and cypress (*Cupressus*) to the fresh tones of lady's mantle (*Alchemilla mollis*) and moluccella (*Moluccella laevis*), or bells of Ireland as it is also called, the variety in shape, shade and size of foliage is enormous.

However, green plant material is not simply confined to trees, hedgerows and grasses, as there are a surprising number of flowers of this colour as well. There are pale and creamy types such as young hydrangeas (*Hydrangea*) – although these may often mature into heads which are pink, blue or white – lilac (*Syringa*), 'Shamrock' chrysanthemums (*Chrysanthemum* 'Shamrock'), large, dahlia-like zinnias (*Zinnia elegans*) and guelder rose (*Viburnum opulus*); the latter have woody stems which should be hammered to help them take up water. While spurge (*Euphorbia*), hellebore (*Helleborus foetidus*), which has deeply veined leaves and bell-shaped blooms, the similar false hellebore (*Veratrum*), with its lance-like leaves and fresh green flower sprays and the large, bushy umbrels of angelica (*Angelica archangelica*) all have more of a lemon or lime colouring.

Other flowers with particularly interesting forms are: 'Lovebird' and 'Orb' auricula primulas (*Primula auricula*) which have green florets surrounding a white eye, and the wonderful velvety love-lies-bleeding (*Amaranthus caudatus* 'Viridis'). You should remove all the leaves from their stems to highlight the electric green drooping tassels. And there are large, flat painter's palettes (*Anthurium*) which blend from green to white, as do 'Green Goddess' arum lilies (*Zantedeschia aethiopica* 'Green Goddess'), although the latter has a soft, floppy texture rather than the stiffer, shiny surface of the former. Some flowers such as Solomon's seal (*Polygonatum*) has graceful, arching stems hung with clusters of small green bells while various types of star of Bethlehem or chincherinchee (*Ornithogalum*) have conical heads of tight green buds which blossom into white. These flowers have a deliciously sweet smell and last for weeks as cut stems.

Greens are a joy to use because they complement almost any other colour in the spectrum.

To begin with there are the possibilities offered by herbs: rosemary (*Rosmarinus officinalis*) is a particularly decorative filler, as is rue (*Ruta graveolens*), although its sap can be an irritant to the skin, so you should wash your hands thoroughly after handling the plant. 'Jackman's Blue' is especially attractive and, like many herbs, dries well. You can make fresh or dried green bunches for the kitchen from sage (*Salvia*), which is blue- or gray-green, dill (*Anethum graveolens*), fennel (*Foeniculum vulgare*) and bay

Green

Right: To construct this large green arrangement, I secured a branch of unripe bananas (Musa) to a solid base, with strong florist's wire. I covered the foot of the base with dried bamboo snake grass (Scirpus tabernaemontani 'Zebrinus'). The stems are supported by wet florist's foam and radiate out from an artichoke (Cynara scolymus). The foliage includes spirals of Bells of Ireland (Moluccella) and tall umbrellas of tropical grass (Cyperus papyrus).

(*Laurus nobilis*). This herb has a long and interesting history; in Medieval times it was used to crown the heads of university graduates, the French term *baccalaureat* and the English "bachelor" which today denote academic success are derivations of the name of the plant. You can decorate foam balls with bay or laurel: the leaves should be young and pliable; wire each leaf individually at its rounded end using a hairpin-shaped piece of wire; continue to add more leaves so that they overlap each other, making sure that none of the foam base is visible; glue any pointed tips of the leaves which

are not secured to the ball; then wrap the ball in tightly tied muslin and leave it to dry out. You can also add a bow or some sprigs of dried flowers to the leaf-covered ball to mai. an original decoration to hang on a Christmas tree.

Greens offer the arranger a rich diversity of forms. Variegated leaves include: ivies (*Hedera*), striped mother-in-law's tongue (*Sansevieria trifasciata*) and snow-on-the-mountain (*Euphorbia marginata*), the latter have sappy stems and should be sealed with either a flame or else with boiling water to improve longevity, and other types of euphorbias also benefit from this treatment, (see Techniques, page 174). Then there are delicate grasses such as bear grass (*Dasylirion*) and papyrus grass (*Cyperus*), feathery ferns and huge, tropical palms, like palm leaf (*Phoenix canariensis*) and banana leaf (*Musa ornata*). Silvery foliage such as pussy willow (*Salix caprea*), catkins, whitebeam (*Sorbus aria*), senecio (*Senecio*), soft furry lamb's ears (*Stachys lanata*) and eucalyptus (*Eucalyptus*), which has a fresh, minty smell, mix particularly well with dusky pinks and blues and tend to envigorate adjacent colours.

One of the most memorable weddings I have ever had the pleasure of arranging the flowers for was an all-green occasion. The bride was getting married immediately after Christmas, at a time of year when, in Britain, it can be difficult to obtain many fresh flowers, and their prices are inflated because of their scarcity. The floral decoration consisted of berried evergreen foliage and mistletoe (*Viscum*) was wired into an attractive bridal bouquet. Green themes, especially if you choose contrasting tones and variegated leaves, can be most original and you should not be afraid to create all-green arrangements, giving them a touch of colouring with berried varieties such as purple barberries (*Berberis*), red skimmia (*Skimmia japonica*) or pinkish cowberries (*Vaccinium vitis idaea*). You can also provide variety of shape and texture by adding vegetables, for instance ornamental cabbages (*Brassica oleracea*) have crinkly cream or pink leaves and look wonderful in a table arrangement; they will not exude any smell unless the room is very warm. Green peppers (*Capsicum*), fresh, hollowed-out pieces of bamboo or the speared heads of plump artichokes (*Cynara scolymus*) all add an interesting touch. In fact there is such an abundance of green-skinned vegetables and fruits that these can be wired into a foam base and adorned with grasses, herbs or fluffy onion heads (*Allium aflatunense*), mixed with a few elaborate flowers, perhaps a few lily heads or lovely green South African proteas (*Protea repens wit*). Choose flat leaves

Fresh greens

1 White beam *(Sorbus aria)*
2 Mother-in-law's tongue
    (Sansevieria trifasciata)
3 Huckleberry *(Gaylussacia)*
4 Eucalyptus *(Eucalyptus gunnii)*
5 Guelder rose *(Viburnum opulus)*
6 Ivy *(Hedera)*
7 Rosemary *(Rosmarinus officinalis)*
8 Grevillea *(Grevillea rosmarinifolia)*
9 'Tineke' rose *(Rosa* 'Tineke'*)*
10 Cowberry *(Vaccinium vitis-idaea)*
11 Bear grass *(Dasylirion)*
12 Foxglove *(Digitalis)*
13 Palm leaf *(Phoenix canariensis)*
14 Lilac *(Syringa)*
15 'White Peacock' lily *(Lilium*
    'White Peacock'*)*
16 Singapore orchid *(Dendrobium*
    fratima)
17 Hebe *(Hebe)*
18 Love-in-a-mist *(Nigella*
    damascena)
19 'Weber Parrot' tulip *(Tulipa*
    'Weber Parrot'*)*
20 'Shamrock' chrysanthemum
    (Chrysanthemum 'Shamrock'*)*
21 Globe artichoke *(Cynara scolymus)*
22 Alstroemeria *(Alstroemeria)*
23 Protea *(Protea repens wit)*
24 'Porcelina' rose *(Rosa* 'Porcelina'*)*
25 Solomon's seal *(Polygonatum)*
26 Mock orange *(Pittosporum tobira)*
27 Arum lily *(Zantedeschia)*
28 Lady's mantle *(Alchemilla mollis)*
29 Butcher's broom *(Ruscus aculeatus)*
30 Dill *(Anethum graveolens)*
31 Bupleurum *(Bupleurum)*
32 Banana leaf *(Musa ornata)*
33 Papyrus grass *(Cyperus)*
34 Moluccella *(Moluccella laevis)*
35 Hosta *(Hosta)*
36 Star of Bethlehem *(Ornithogalum)*
37 Star of Bethlehem 'Mount
    Everest' *(Ornithogalum arabicum*
    'Mount Everest'*)*
38 Onion head *(Allium aflatunense)*
39 Trachelium *(Trachelium)*
40 Fern *(Asparagus sprengeri)*
41 Tree fern *(Asparagus pyramidalis)*
42 Snow-on-the-mountain
    (Euphorbia marginata)
43 Anemone *(Anemone)*
44 'Christmas Beauty' orchid
    (Cymbidium 'Christmas Beauty'*)*
45 Painter's palette *(Anthurium)*
46 Eucalyptus *(Eucalyptus)*
47 Star of Bethlehem *(Ornithogalum*
    thyrsoides)
48 Fern *(Asparagus plumosa)*
49 'Revue' chrysanthemum
    (Chrysanthemum 'Revue'*)*
50 'Fiori' lily *(Lilium* 'Fiori'*)*

such as hosta *(Hosta)* – which comes in attractive variegated varieties – or galax *(Galax)* to provide a "ruff" around table arrangements, using their large surfaces to cover any mechanics. Galax leaves are something of a mystery: they are flown in from Florida but are in fact grown in the wild; if you keep these leaves in a box lined with damp paper they will live without water for a very long time. Their distinct heart shapes makes them ideal for fringing a posy of flowers as a Valentine's Day or a Mother's Day gift.

There are a few green plants illustrated in this book which deserve a special mention. First, the pitcher plant *(Sarracenia)* which is an insectivore. Originally from the marshy coastland areas of North and South America, its trumpet leaves have a hooded top which traps prey. These unusual flowers require large amounts of water and benefit from cut-flower feed. They are cultivated in the Netherlands and also by some small, specialist nurseries. Because they are not grown on a large scale they are relatively expensive to buy, however, they are sure to be noticed, (see page 113). Second, the East India lotus *(Nelumbo nucifera)*, which in fact originates in Egypt, where it is still grown and harvested. The leaves are a fantastic green colour, (see page 1), and dry well placed in a warm room with their stalks pointing upward; once they have lost their moisture you can make magical dried arrangements with them. East India lotus seedheads also dessicate easily, although you may need to attach them to an artificial stem such as a green garden cane, bound with florist's tape, before adding them to an arrangement. Third, the dried aniseed-scented giant hog weed *(Heracleum mantegazzianum)* which can reach a height of 12ft (3m). It grows in marshy places and is particularly apt for a party setting. Many people are allergic to its sap, but when dried it makes a harmless plant decoration which is interesting to look at, (see page 61).

Some of the most extraordinary green-hued flowers belong to the orchid family, and they are also some of the rarest and consequently most expensive varieties. While 'Singapore' *(Dendrobium fratima)* and 'Christmas Beauty' orchids *(Cymbidium* 'Christmas Beauty'*)* are more common, the

'Green Slipper' orchid *(Paphiopedilum)* is rather more unusual, (see page 1), and deserves to steal the show in any arrangement. For this reason do not mix it with other stems so that the exquisite markings on the petals remain prominent. Because of its hairy stem it will not thrive in deep water, but these flowers will keep for up to six weeks if looked after properly. As is often the case, the most highly price blooms are worth their expense because they last so well. Also, you should be careful not to allow moisture to come into contact with the petals of orchids, so in particular avoid using a mister spray to dampen the flowers. Far from reviving them, as is the case with other varieties, water even in a gentle spray form will quickly make the petals turn limp and translucent.

Remember that some flowers – prime example being lilies *(Lilium)* – have plenty of lush foliage on their stems, so there is no need to add any extraneous leaf to stems such as these as it will only swamp the overall effect. Although it is advisable to remove the leaves low down on cut stems before arranging (as they can get in the way of mechanics such as chicken or mesh wire and also add unnecessary bulk to the stems inside a container) you should not remove the leaves on the upper stem – these will always enhance the blooms on the stem. Choosing leafy stalks is also an easy way to economize on obtaining additional foliage. All sorts of green leaf varieties and some green flowers are illustrated on page 88-9.

Above left: A sheaf of various grasses, slender bamboo, lavender (Lavandula), green poppy (Papaver) seedheads and fennel (Foeniculum) tied with a "tail" of hanging amaranthus (Amaranthus caudatus). To make a sheaf-like bunch see Techniques, page 175.
Above right: You can adapt an egg-collecting basket to hold flowers: wedge a water-filled vessel inside it with moss. Then fill the inner container with eucalyptus (Eucalyptus), spiraea (Spiraea), pittosporum (Pittosporum), copper beech (Fagus sylvatica purpurea) and sorbus (Sorbus) and take some painter's palettes (Anthurium) to act as focal flowers.
Right: Hosta (Hosta) leaves disguise a bucket holding a rich variety of dense foliage.
Overleaf: An old tree root covered with decorative and edible plant material.

Although there are relatively fewer types of commercially grown blue flowers than there are red, yellow or white varieties, the spectrum of light blues and pale mauves to deep azures and sumptuous purples offers flower arrangers all kinds of interesting possibilities. Blue is a so-called "cool" colour which "recedes" when mixed with other, warmer hues. For this reason, blues look their best either in a mono-chromatic arrangement or else mixed with other shades which will not deaden their impact. However, this is not a limitation, as with a little imagination they can create a host of different moods. For example, purple is a majestic colour and tall, massed delphiniums *(Delphinium)* or larkspur *(Delphinium consolida)* can look very stately. These showy flowers are most effective arranged in a large vase and they make beautiful church decoration. To highlight the blues in a dark setting or under artificial light it is best to mix in some white stems. If you are using spikes of delphiniums for a special occasion it is beneficial to fill the hollow stems with water and then plug the ends with cotton wool – this will ensure that they remain fresh (see page 174). For general use you should give them a long drink in deep water before you begin arranging. The richness of purples and deep blues strike a grand note, perhaps because of their lingering historical associations with royalty; these dyes were once an expensive rarity and only the most privileged classes could afford them. At the opposite end of the scale, the intense blues of cornflowers, or knapweed as they are also called *(Centaurea cyanus)*, or the sky-blue of spiderwort *(Tradescantia)*, with its delicate three-petalled blooms, can be arranged simply in a small jug or crock.

There are numerous blue flowers which are particularly charming because of their simplicity and miniature scale. Such blooms include the aptly named Canterbury bells *(Campanula medium)*, catmint *(Nepeta)*, with its lavender-tinted flowers and aromatic foliage, pretty perennial flax *(Linum perenne)*, once grown as the raw material for Irish linen and wild bluebells *(Endymion nonscriptus)*, which carpet woodlands in the spring in northern climes. Many people find wild bluebells very short-lived once brought indoors. However, this is usually because their stems are picked too long. If you pick them no longer than 4in (10cm) and mass them tightly in a small container then they will last well and smell delicious. Because the stems droop quickly once cut, you can wrap them in polythene or paper to prevent this. Small blooms such as these are particularly appropriate for constructing posies

which make ideal gifts: they require relatively few stems and can be created by adults and children to all sorts of colour schemes, taking into account the recipient's favourite varieties. I like to use grape hyacinths *(Muscari)* mixed with cowslip *(Primula veris)* or diminutive pink 'Serena' roses *(Rosa 'Serena')*.

On February 14, Saint Valentine's Day, I vary the traditional theme of romantic red, and blend crimson spray roses with lily-of-the-valley *(Convallaria majalis)* and forget-me-nots

Blue

Right: A large, heavy urn provides a stable base for a dense and lavish spray of tall delphiniums (Delphinium). I lined the container with a bucket and filled the latter with water. Delphiniums are available in a broad spectrum of complementary colours: whites, pinks, mauves, purples and blues all blend naturally with each other. As an alternative you can use spirals of giant larkspur (Consolida ambigua) or else stems of veronica (Veronica).

(Myosotis) in a red, white and blue scheme. Violets *(Viola odorata)*, with their heady scent, wonderful rich purple colouring and velvety texture, are also suitable to include in posies, although sadly these do not last well once cut. You should keep them cool to improve long-evity and if the petals are wilting you can plunge the whole flower into cool water for up to half an hour to revive them (see Techniques, page 174). Delicate star-shaped brodiaeas *(Brodiaea)* are another alternative; they are available most of the year around and last very well, flowering for up to three weeks.

There are also plenty of long-stemmed blue flowers to arrange with, including fragrant lilac *(Syringa)*, and the similar-looking buddleia *(Buddleia)*. Both lose some of their aroma once they have been cut, but their long stems with clusters of tiny blooms are useful for providing an outline in large-scale displays. Mauve and purple buddleia combine well with other pink and blue blooms, and you should dip the ends of the stems in boiling water to help the flowers drink. Cultivated lilac should be placed in water containing a suitable commercial cut-flower feed which helps to prolong the life of their woody stems. You should also remove nearly all the foliage from the stems which otherwise deprives the flower heads of water. Also, hammer the ends of the stems well and dip them in boiling water to help the plant take up water (see Techniques, page 174). Commer-cially produced lilac has much less scent than the home-grown garden variety, and sweet peas *(Lathyrus odoratus)* grown for the flower market suffer in just the same way. The most fragrant sweet pea is the old-fashioned mauve type.

I also like to use agapanthus or African lilies *(Agapanthus africanus)* as they are also called, which have tall, smooth stems and big, deep-blue flowering umbrels and fluffy, round onion heads *(Allium aflatunense)*. You should avoid placing the stems of onion heads in warm water as this will bring out their smell; by adding a drop of household bleach to cold water you can prevent any odour emanating from the arrangement. Phlox *(Phlox)*, the profuse heads of hydrangeas *(Hydrangea macrophylla)* or the elegant stems of irises *(Iris)* – my favourite is the deep purple 'Professor Blauw' variety – provide more options. Irises tend not last well, but to improve their longevity you can cut the ends of the stems on a slant (see Techniques, page 174) and remove each flower as it fades to encourage the next buds to open. Phlox are lovely to arrange with and you should remove the petals as they begin to drop to prevent the sprays from looking faded long before they are over. Hydrangeas add density to any large group of flowers and are as attractive fresh as they are dried. The "*hydro*" part of their name is a hint that these plants require a great deal of water. You can plunge their entire heads into water to revive them (see Techniques, page 174). They are also easy flowers to dry: simply remove the foliage and leave them in a very warm place such as an airing cupboard: the quicker they dry, the better colour they seem to keep. You should not hang them upside down as they dry better with the ends of their stems standing in shallow water and their heads exposed to warm air.

Majestic blues

1 Cornflower
   (Centaurea cyanus)
2 Cottage scabious *(Scabiosa)*
3 Scabious *(Scabiosa)*
4 Trachelium *(Trachelium)*
5 Gay feathers *(Liatris)*
6 Phlox *(Phlox)*
7 'Blue Heaven' freesia *(Freesia 'Blue Heaven')*
8 'Blue Moon' rose *(Rosa 'Blue Moon')*
9 Veronica *(Veronica)*
10 Daisy *(Osteospermum)*
11 Globe artichoke
   (Cynara scolymus)
12 Sweet pea
   (Lathyrus odoratus)
13 Buddleia *(Buddleia)*
14 Sea lavender *(Limonium)*
15 Lobelia *(Lobelia)*
16 Anemone *(Anemone)*
17 Brodiaea *(Brodiaea)*
18 Gentian *(Gentiana)*
19 Michaelmas daisy
   (Aster albescens)
20 Globe thistle *(Echinops)*
21 Monkshood *(Aconitum)*
22 Delphinium
   (Delphinium elatum)
23 Larkspur
   (Delphinium consolida)
24 Gladiolus *(Gladioulus)*
25 Lisianthus *(Eustoma)*
26 'Blue Bees' delphinium
   (Delphinium belladonna 'Blue Bees')
27 Seaholly *(Eryngium)*

Other softer-hued flowers such as cottage scabious *(Scabiosa)*, which last well, and the wispy love-in-a-mist *(Nigella damascena)* combine well with creams, whites and gentle pinks. The unusual spiky flower heads of Scotch or cotton thistles *(Onopordum acanthium)* are fun to use when working to a modern theme, as long as you wear gloves to protect your hands! If you cannot obtain thistles, then the larger heads of globe artichokes *(Cynara scolymus)* are a good alternative – these mix well with branches of tortured willow *(Salix matsudana* 'Tortuosa'*)*. I also like the gray-blue heads of globe thistles *(Echinops)* and sea holly *(Eryngium)*; both of these varieties are complemented by soft pinks or strong reds.

During the months of the year when many cut flowers are out of season and therefore expensive to buy, you can create arrangements by planting bulbs such as scilla or squill *(Scilla)* in moist peat moss, although you will have to wait for some weeks before the brilliant blue flowers appear. Most bulbs take a couple of months to bloom, but florists nowadays sell them on the point of bursting into flower. Hyacinths *(Hyacinthus orientalis)* grow well indoors when planted in shallow bowls, or you can set a single bulb in a glass hyacinth container – the design of these attractive vases is based on old botanical specimen jars – so that you can see the roots of the bulb under the water. I often put a bowlful of hyacinths in my bathroom where it acts as the most heavenly natural air freshener.

Because of the relatively few varieties of blue cut flowers, some florists resort to dyeing blooms. You should be aware that some "blue" chrysanthemums *(Chrysanthemum)*, carnations *(Dianthus)* and gypsophila *(Gypsophila)* have absorbed dyed water through their stems. Intriguing as this tinting method may be, I much prefer to use flowers of a natural hue, as it seems a shame to choose artificial colours when there are real blues available. I am particularly fond of the natural, vivid colour of gentians *(Gentiana)*. For years I bought these flowers although I felt very frustrated that they refused to open fully, even when I patiently coaxed them in a

warm room. Whatever advice I sought, they stayed resolutely in bud. One day I read an American folk story about three fairies who took shelter from the rain inside the head of a gentian, and from this tale I learned that the flowers, even if they appear to be on the verge of blossoming, will rarely become full-blown; the species are only pollinated by very persistent bumble bees! Nevertheless, gentians are worth buying not only for their beauty but because they last well, even if their petals remain semi-closed!

There are no strict rules about which colours do or do not combine well with blues. You cannot go far wrong adding whites or creams, perhaps as a simple duo-tone bunch of scabious *(Scabiosa)* or else tall spires of delphiniums *(Delphinium)*. Often you will find that a little experimentation pays off and an addition of strong yellows and even vivid shades of orange or bright reds can also create a striking effect. On the whole, pinks blend successfully with blues, particularly the paler shades, and silvery foliage mixes well with mauve. Although certain flowers such as roses – with the exception of the lovely 'Blue Moon' rose *(Rosa* 'Blue Moon'*)* – are not available in blue, plenty of other varieties compensate. Look for anemones *(Anemone)*, and the quite beautiful and somewhat poppy-like lisianthus *(Eustoma)* which come in strong purply-blues, many of which, far from being receding and "cool", are rich, eye-catching shades. There is a selection of rich blues and purples on pages 96–7.

Above left: Sweet peas (Lathyrus odoratus), veronica (Veronica), lady's mantle (Alchemilla mollis), Canterbury bells (Campanula medium), eucalyptus (Eucalyptus) and scabius (Scabiosa) arranged in an informal spray in a small frosted-glass vase.
Above right: A sweet-scented posy of violet (Viola) blooms, fringed with their own leaves.
Right: This modern display is composed of onion heads (Allium sphaerocephalon), aechmea leaves (Aechmea fasciata), globe thistles (Echinops), sea holly (Eryngium), contorted poppy (Papaver), teasels (Dipsacus) and a bright-pink curacoa flower native to Thailand.
Overleaf: In this blue-theme arrangement the crossed stems in the vase support each other.

Although white is not a real colour, it is a shade which offers the flower arranger enormous scope. It has long been associated with purity and innocence, and is an equally suitable choice for celebratory as well as sympathy flowers. Vita Sackville-West, the pioneering English gardener, said: "I love colour and rejoice in it, but white is lovely for me forever." This is a sentiment which many people share, and whatever the charms of other "real" colours, white has universal appeal because it is so versatile.

There are all sorts of beautiful white blooms available to flower arrangers which are not only "cool" and serene, but also soothing to look at. Pure whites, or those tinged with blue or green are "cooler" than creams, which often contain a hint of yellow or pink. All these variations have a high level of luminosity and are as appropriate in an informal setting as they are in a formal one. Because whites and creams reflect light so effectively they are particularly suitable in dark interiors, such as religious buildings. They are also ideal set in the middle of an evening dinner table, and under soft lighting, or in the glow of candles, the petals are highlighted to their best advantage. The neutrality of white gives it great versatility and not only is it a safe choice for most settings, but it also works well in almost any kind of container. However, very pale blooms in a white container may look somewhat insipid and colourless.

One of the flowers most immediately associated with white is the trumpet or Easter lily *(Lilium longiflorum)*. These graceful stems are widely cultivated and bear a close resemblance to the original "lily of the field" or Madonna lily *(Lilium candidum)*. The latter is a common feature in paintings depicting the Annunciation. Lilies have been the chosen flowers of altars the world over for centuries and they are potent spiritual symbols at Eastertide and for weddings. Their exquisite petals and arched stems give them a very special aesthetic quality. Added to this they have the advantage of showing up well from a long distance – an important asset for special occasion flowers – and they also last longer in water than almost any other cut flower. White is still the predominant colour for weddings in the Western world. Lilies are archetypal bridal flowers and combine well with, for example, creamy 'Tineke' roses *(Rosa* 'Tineke') or 'White Dream' roses *(Rosa* 'White Dream') and pale freesias *(Freesia)*. You can wire them into a cascading shower bouquet with lily-of-the-valley *(Convallaria majalis)* and trails of ivy *(Hedera)* to make a sweet-smelling monochromatic display. The simplest and perhaps most attractive way to

appreciate lily-of-the-valley, which otherwise tends to be swamped by larger blooms, is to make a posy in your hand and surround it with a frill of its own leaves. Most commercially available lily-of-the-valley has been forced and is rather fragile; to protect the flowers you can wrap them in tissue paper and leave them overnight in deep water before arranging them.

A high proportion of white flowers are scented and there are two particularly pungent varieties. First, tuberoses *(Polianthes tuberosa)*,

White

Right: This trumpet-shaped glass vase lends itself well to freshly cut stems. Here I have combined bellflowers (Campanula), delphiniums (Delphinium), trachelium (Trachelium), 'Tineke' roses (Rosa 'Tineke'), peonies (Paeonia) and 'Casablanca' lilies (Lilium 'Casablanca') with eucalyptus (Eucalyptus) and butcher's broom (Ruscus). Make sure that a glass container is clean before arranging, or the effect of the display will be spoiled.

which are cultivated mainly in France, Israel and South Africa. Even though these are not spectacular blooms they lend a wonderful fragrance when mixed with other flowers. You can also remove the star-shaped blooms from their stems to decorate a bride's or a bridesmaid's headdress. Second, stephanotis *(Stephanotis)* which has scented, waxy flowers. These are often sold insulated under plastic and must be arranged as soon as they have been purchased. Otherwise, you can stretch some tissue paper over a shallow bowl half-filled with water and secure it with string so that it is taut. Then

make holes in the paper and insert the flower stems – this prevents the waxy flowers from touching the water, which would quickly turn them brown. Conditioned like this, stephanotis should last the length of a wedding day. You can also buy them in a less perishable form as potted plants which twine around wooden canes. You can cut blooms off the plant and use them for delicate bridal work. You can construct a monochromatic arrangement on any scale. Miniature flowers such as scill or squill *(Scilla)*, bluebells *(Hyacinthoides)* and snowdrops *(Galanthus)* – so-called because they sometimes bloom when there is snow on the ground – look pretty grown from bulbs in a bowl or as cut stems bunched together informally in a small vase or in an adapted receptacle such as a teacup or a perfume bottle. White cyclamen *(Cyclamen)* are popular potted flowers, but as with other flowering pot plants they often perish due to over-watering. To keep cyclamen healthy you should wait until the leaves are almost starting to wilt before watering them. I have even heard of people giving them cold tea every few days with good results!

For a large-scale display use mop-headed hydrangeas *(Hydrangea macrophylla)*, full-blown 'Cassa' chrysanthemums *(Chrysanthemum* 'Cassa'), 'Eveline' dahlias *(Dahlia* 'Eveline'), onion heads *(Allium aflatunense)*, 'Teach In' gladioli *(Gladiolus* 'Teach In') or bridal gladioli *(Gladiolus colvillei)*, blended with dark foliage to provide contrast to the pale petals. You should always remove the dead flowers on a gladiolus stem so that the rest of the buds will open properly. Other varieties such as 'White Velleta' gerberas *(Gerbera* 'White Velleta'), 'Mona Lisa' alstroemerias *(Alstroemeria* 'Mona Lisa'), 'Bianca Charmeur' carnations *(Dianthus* 'Bianca Charmeur') and 'Pax' tulips *(Tulipa* 'Pax') arranged in a loose spray in a vase provide attractive, medium-sized bunches.

There are also many types of useful "filler" flowers, which give a display body in the same way as foliage. Particularly suitable are the feathery stems of love-in-a-mist *(Nigella damascena)*, dill *(Anethum graveolens)*, feverfew *(Chrysanthemum parthenium)*, 'Monte Cassino' aster *(Aster* 'Monte Cassino'), loosestrife *(Lysimachia)* and gypsophila *(Gypsophila)*. The latter is very popular as it is simultaneously bushy and delicate; the pretty white flowers also die without drooping and dry well. Unfortunately the stems often get tangled during transportation. However, a full vase of dense, fluffy gypsophila is a joy to behold. I often use seasonal soapwort *(Saponaria vaccaria)* for the same purpose; it has a similar appearance, but

Elegant whites

1 Alstroemeria *(Alstroemeria)*
2 Silk weed *(Asclepias physocarpa)*
3 Easter lily *(Lilium longiflorum)*
4 Love-in-a-mist *(Nigella damascena)*
5 'Eveline' dahlia *(Dahlia 'Eveline')*
6 Painter's palette *(Anthurium)*
7 Statice *(Limonium sinuatum)*
8 'Bianca' carnation *(Dianthus 'Bianca')*
9 'Madame Wit' orchid *(Dendrobium 'Madame Wit')*
10 White buttons *(Chrysanthemum parthenium)*
11 Dahlia *(Dahlia)*
12 Feverfew *(Chrysanthemum parthenium)*
13 Gypsophila *(Gypsophila)*
14 'Ludwig Dazzler' amaryllis *(Hippeastrum 'Ludwig Dazzler')*
15 Star of Bethlehem *(Ornithogalum arabicum)*
16 Scabious *(Scabiosa)*
17 'White Velleta' gerbera *(Gerbera 'White Velleta')*
18 'Pax' tulip *(Tulipa 'Pax')*
19 Delphinium *(Delphinium elatum)*
20 Chimney bellfower *(Campanula pyramidalis)*
21 African lily *(Agapanthus africanus)*
22 Onion head *(Allium aflatunense)*
23 Stock *(Matthiola)*
24 Dill *(Anethum graveolens)*
25 'Tineke' rose *(Rosa 'Tineke')*
26 'The Bride' orchid *(Cymbidium 'The Bride')*
27 'Bianca Charmeur' carnation *(Dianthus 'Bianca Charmeur')*
28 Loosestrife *(Lysimachia)*
29 Orchid *(Phalaenopsis)*
30 Bridal gladiolus *(Gladiolus colvillei)*
31 Arum lily *(Zantedeschia)*
32 'White Dream' rose *(Rosa 'White Dream')*
33 'Cassa' chrysanthemum *(Chrysanthemum 'Cassa')*
34 Star of Bethlehem *(Ornithogalum thyrsoides)*
35 Lisianthus *(Eustoma grandiflorum)*
36 'Monte Cassino' aster *(Aster 'Monte Cassino')*
37 Larkspur *(Delphinium consolida)*
38 'Teach In' gladiolus *(Gladiolus 'Teach In')*
39 Foxtail lily *(Eremurus himalaicus)*
40 Larkspur *(Delphinium consolida)*
41 Delphinium *(Delphinium elatum)*
42 Larkspur *(Delphinium consolida)*
43 Snapdragon *(Antirrhinum majus)*
44 Bouvardia *(Bouvardia)*
45 'Casablanca' lily *(Lilium 'Casablanca')*

I like to blend creams and whites with pinks and blues and set these colours off with a silvery foliage such as senecio *(Senecio)*, artemisia *(Artemisia ludoviciana)*, cotton lavender *(Santolina chamaecyparissus)* or eucalyptus leaves *(Eucalyptus)*. Gray or silver foliage is useful for heightening the colours of other blooms and conversely, a bright green such as elder *(Sambucus)* or elaeagnus *(Elaeagnus pungens)* will deaden the impression of colourful petals. I also like to mix blue larkspur *(Delphinium consolida)* with pale pinks, cerise pinks and dark reds of the same variety, and set off these combined colours with young green foliage such as lady's mantle *(Alchemilla mollis)* or moluccella or bells of Ireland *(Moluccella laevis)* as they are also known as.

I often choose strong shades of blue and mauve and mix them with green and white when I am commissioned to decorate office interiors, as open-plan, brightly lit areas show off these colours to their best advantage. Conversely, I rarely select these hues when decorating a dark interior such as a religious building, as in dimly lit conditions, especially under stained-glass windows, blues appear to recede and lose much of their impact. Personally, I prefer not to mix yellow with pink, although a combination of a bright yellow and a bright pink can be suitable for a party or tropical-style arrangement such as my tablescape (see page 40-1).

As well as the all-important consideration of colour, the shape and size of plant material play a role in creating a harmonious display. For instance, bright tropical flowers such as painter's palettes *(Anthurium)*, heliconias *(Heliconia)* and proteas *(Protea)* will not harmonize with more temperate garden flowers such as roses *(Rosa)* and daffodils *(Narcissus)*. So it is necessary to gauge the mood of different blooms and match them accordingly. Orchids are particularly difficult to blend with other varieties. They are often so intricate and unusual in form that they invariably work most effectively arranged on their own.

Another useful technique for mixing flowers is to group stems of the same variety and colour together. Whether you are constructing a wreath, a bunch or a bouquet, grouping will provide a much stronger visual impact, particularly in the case of small and delicate flowers. Do not overlook the chromatic versatility of fruits and vegetables in flower arranging, as they provide all sorts of interesting shapes, textures and hues. As well as foliage, dried flowers are a useful means of lessening the impact of bright flowers. Whether you dry your own cut flowers by hanging them upside down in a warm place such as an airing cupboard, or buy them direct from a florist, the tones of dried stems are naturally faded and gentle and so neutralize the strength of fresher blooms. However, today many dried varieties are dyed so that they have artificially bold hues.

Whether you choose to mix flowers of different colours by closely complementing shades of one colour or by boldly contrasting colours such as yellow and purple, red and blue or pink and orange, you should always be guided by your own eye. As you work, you can remove colours which jar, break up patches of colour which are too strong with foliage or duller hues or add a dash of bold colouring if you feel the display is lacking impact. Mixing, in other words, is a question of judging the effect of the arrangement as you create it.

Above left: Lotus (Nelumbo) flowers ringed with the vivid hues of solidaster (Solidaster), lady's mantle (Alchemilla mollis) and matricaria (Chrysanthemum parthenium).
Above right: Chicken or mesh wire moulded into a cone-shaped frame and covered with moss and then decorated with colourful miniature tropical fruits and small-headed flowers.
Right: Groups of white, purple and yellow irises (Iris) arranged around an insectivore, the pitcher plant (Sarracenia). 'Moonshine' achillea (Achillea 'Moonshine') fringes the vase.
Overleaf: An informal spray of mixed flowers arranged loosely in a beehive pot.

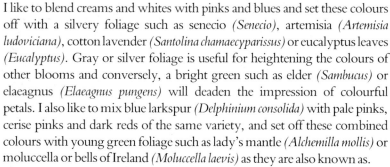

The enormous variety of plant materials available today offers the arranger an almost limitless array of colours. Nature's rich palette is forever being expanded by skilled plant breeders and hybridizers so that the myriad colours on the market leave flower-lovers spoilt for choice. Colours are fundamental to our appreciation of flowers, but the perception of colours and how to combine them is highly subjective; this will be immediately obvious to you if you browse through publications on flower arranging.

Despite the many theories on mixing and matching colours, the most important rule to my mind is that you should arrange flowers which *you* think complement and contrast most effectively with each other. Although colour choice is largely a matter of personal taste and therefore evades strict dos and don'ts, there is still plenty of room for novices and more experienced flower arrangers to learn: the more you experiment with flowers the more you will discover what your own likes and dislikes are when it comes to colour themes.

The simplest way to start mixing flowers is to blend different shades of the same species together. For instance, a blue and white spray of delphiniums *(Delphinium)* or irises *(Iris)* or cream and yellow daffodils *(Narcissus)*. If you choose green or white as part of a duo-tone theme then you cannot go far wrong as both these hues neutralize other primary and secondary colours. However, you do need to create a visual balance both in terms of colour and in the size and shape and overall proportion of your chosen flowers. Experiment using one dominant colour with an infill of, for instance, white or green, and then reverse this approach. Once you have established a colour scheme you like you can deepen the overall effect by adding darker shades, or lighten it with paler tints, in particular white or cream.

If you are sending a gift to someone through a relay florist service then you may have to place an order over the telephone. In which case it is often safer to ask for a two-colour arrangement; this will probably be much more attractive than the rather garish multi-coloured displays that many commercial florists produce. To my mind these often look as if there has been little thought paid to the colour scheme.

As a guideline I suggest that you match flowers as you please, but pay close attention to proportion and aim to mix your selected colours in roughly equal amounts. If you use one hue too dominantly in a very mixed arrangement then the whole will lack harmony. And if you think your display is looking too brash then you can always add foliage to tone down the visual effect. I particularly like to mix colours when creating an informal, country-style display, using garden or wild flowers. In temperate zones these generally have softer hues and it is quite difficult to find shades which clash. In contrast, many commercial and hybrid varieties are much less subtle. Blooms cultivated for the floristry trade usually have little or

Mixed Colours

Right: A riotous display of mixed colours, arranged in a container covered with sunflower (Helianthus) seedheads. The flowers include wiry orange banksia (Banksia coccinea), fluffy celosia (Celosia), heliconias (Heliconia), leucospernum (Leucospernum cordifolium), arum lilies (Zantedeschia) and proteas (Protea). The bright orange and yellow theme is well-complemented by the use of brown glycerined foliage and Bells of Ireland (Moluccella laevis).

no foliage on their stems. They have been bred in this way so that the flower heads grow stronger and larger and a minimum amount of energy goes into the growth of the leaves. You will notice that with home-grown varieties there is much more greenery on the stems.

Mixing colours depends to some extent on the seasonal availability of blooms. As the year unfolds I tend to adopt different colour themes, although there are some species such as roses *(Rosa)*, lilies *(Lilium)* and gerberas *(Gerbera)* which I rely on throughout the year. In the spring I often work with yellows and whites. In the summer I enjoy combining pinks and blues, in the autumn or fall I select lots of oranges, blues and reds and during the winter months my favourite combination is red and green. During the weeks before Christmas I use plenty of foliage livened up with nuts, pine cones, fruit, vegetables and all sorts of decorative inorganic items garnered from markets and shops. Much as I enjoy working with reds and whites, which are particularly suitable shades at Christmas, this combination has unpleasant connotations for some people. Although red is the traditional colour of sympathy in Western cultures, red flowers are not always welcome in hospitals, particularly when combined with white blooms, for the obvious reason that these colours have associations with sickness and suffering. In order to get around this taboo you should mix red with a variety of other colours when making an arrangement for someone in hospital, so that it carries no unfavourable symbolism.

Some flowers, such as poppies *(Papaver)*, zinnias *(Zinnia)* and ranunculus *(Ranunculus)* come in all sorts of colours – yellows, oranges, reds and whites – and look charming in a multi-coloured bunch. Ranunculus is one of my very favourite varieties and I am always grateful to the Cornish and the Italians of San Remo, both of whom grow so many. Nothing gives me more pleasure than a bowlful of mixed ranunculus and it is the only type of flower I cannot resist taking home from my shop. I first saw these flowers in a shop window high up in the Swiss Alps and the impression of those vivid petals against gleaming white snowfields has stayed with me. One great advantage of ranunculus is that they take a long time to pass their peak and even once their petals have begun to wither and turn translucent they are still lovely to behold. Sweet peas *(Lathyrus odoratus)* also come in a tantalizing selection of of colours and the gentle shades of pink, white, blue and purple blend happily together.

By studying the colours of individual flowers you can see how Nature mixes certain shades. For example, look at a pansy *(Viola)* and experiment on the theme of purple and yellow. Perhaps create a display of yellow lilies, mauve lisianthus *(Eustoma)*, blue tracheliums *(Trachelium)* and take solidaster *(Solidaster)* as infill flowers. The blue and orange colours which are shown in birds of paradise *(Strelitzia reginae)* may inspire you to mix the globe artichokes *(Cynara scolymus)* with orange gerberas *(Gerbera)*.

Special
Occasions

Flowers are part of our lives from the cradle to the grave and one of the great pleasures of working with flowers is that they accompany us through all the special occasions in life. From the birth of a baby, through christenings, bar mitzvahs, birthdays, weddings, anniversaries and finally as gifts to those sadly departed, flowers in all their versatility can convey messages suited to all kinds of important events.

Special occasions provide us with an opportunity to be a little extravagant and adventurous with flowers. If you grow your own flowers then you will have a ready source of plant material in your garden, otherwise you can buy commercially grown flowers from florists and flower markets. When I am asked to prepare a special gift for someone I always try to gain some insight into the personality of the recipient – how old they are, what their favourite flowers and colours are and what the eventual setting of the blooms will be. The character of the person you are giving to, or the nature of the special occasion you are celebrating, will influence your choice of flowers and foliage. For example, flowers for a religious ceremony will be more formal than those for a birthday, when you can afford to be bold and inventive.

Celebrating special occasions means more than creating gifts for friends and relatives, although there are all kinds of opportunities throughout the year for giving, from personal celebrations such as moving into a new home, achieving success in an exam or at work, getting engaged or making a debut as a performer, to the popular calendar traditions such as Mother's Day, Father's Day and Saint Valentine's Day. Annual celebrations such as Christmas, New Year, Easter, Thanksgiving and Halloween are all times of the year when you can enhance a setting with flowers following some of the basic techniques for arranging described in this book and using some of the relevant equipment shown at the back of the book (see pages 172-9). Flowers are also popular on Saints' days, for example, on St David's Day in Wales daffodils (Narcissus) abound and the shamrock is traditional on St Patrick's Day among Irish communities.

At Christmas, and also at other times of the year such as Harvest Festival, I particularly like constructing garlands. Garlands are an ancient form of flower decoration and one of the earliest recorded examples dates from the 14th century BC when floral remnants were discovered in Tutankhamen's tomb in Egypt which was excavated in 1922. Garlands are time-consuming to make but highly decorative and festive; you can use a large piece of heavy rope as a base, or else build up a chain of grouped bunches of foliage, as illustrated in the Christmas garland on page 137.

New Year is celebrated at different times of the calendar year by different cultures. For instance, during the Chinese New Year, which is celebrated all over the world by Chinese communities, orange trees and blossom are the favoured flower decoration. Because the New Year marks a fresh start I like to use pure white and cream flowers to signify newness, along with plenty of foliage. For centuries decorating with foliage has been traditional during the winter season, in fact since the Middle Ages evergreens have been associated with winter festivals as they are regarded as symbols of survival. In the winter I tend to combine green and red and I like to incorporate candles into my arrangements as the soft light and warmth they emit are appropriate for the long, dark wintry evenings we have in the northern hemisphere.

By contrast, Easter in northern climes coincides with the start of spring and is a time of year when plants are in bud and trees in blossom. At this lovely time of year Nature is bursting into life after the dormancy of winter and the sunny colours of spring flowers certainly help to raise the spirits. Flowers such as daffodils (Narcissus), blue bells (Hyacinthoides), primroses (Primula vulgaris), grape hyacinths (Muscari), forsythia (Forsythia) and lovely magnolia blossom (Magnolia), as well as all sorts of bulbs, are in abundance and consequently their prices drop, making them all the more desirable. For Easter you can line a twig basket with moss or else fashion your own basket from chicken or mesh wire and straw or dried grasses and fill it with eggs and yellow flower heads such as polyanthus (Primula) or chrysanthemums (Chrysanthemum), for instance 'Reyellow', 'Buttercup' or 'Yellow Nikita' varieties. Then you can hard-boil eggs or else blow them (to do this carefully prick both top and bottom with a large needle and blow through one hole, so forcing the liquid white and yolk out of the hole at the opposite end) before painting them with colours which complement your chosen flowers. In Scandanavian countries there is a tradition of creating Easter trees: take long twigs of contorted willow (Salix matsudana 'Tortuosa') and thread cotton through holes made in either end of painted blown eggs with a needle and attach them to the tree.

Decorating religious buildings and other sites for special ceremonies is particularly enjoyable as the flowers will delight your guests and the congregation that follow. And the buildings often provide scope for inventive arrangements. For instance, you can fill a font with flowers arranged in a container filled with water and crumpled large-gauge chicken or mesh wire and trail strands of ivy (Hedera) over the rim. Or you can embellish pew ends with hanging bunches or place large-scale pedestals beside the altar. And a garland framing a porch, gateway or an entrance arch will be a welcome note to guests.

Different species of flowers are regarded as out of the ordinary across the world, and common varieties in some countries are seen as highly unusual in others. Chrysanthemums (Chrysanthemum) are revered in Japan, blossom is particularly sought-after in China and in many Christian parts of the world the lily (Lilium) is regarded as especially pure and serene. Lovely as lilies are (and most varieties are worth their expense because they last well), perhaps the most special flowers you can obtain for an important occasion are orchids. These come in literally thousands of different varieties and forms. Many are magically beautiful and others are quite extraordinary to behold, but however delicate or bizarre they may appear, many are in fact hardy and last well. I particularly like phalaenopsis orchids (Phalaenopsis) and cymbidiums (Cymbidium), which come in numerous shades of yellows, creams, reds and pinks, some with spots, spatters and other unusual markings.

Whatever the reason for your special occasion, you can create apt displays based around candle sticks and candelabra, or you can combine potted and freshly cut blooms in a Pot-et-Fleur arrangement. Or you can construct wreaths using seasonal plant material. For instance, if you look at the selection of floral rings illustrated on pages 116-7 you will see how versatile this form of flower arranging can be. From left to right, I made a spring wreath combining individually wired paper whites (Narcissus 'Paper White') with yellow 'Baroque' roses (Rosa 'Baroque') and variegated euonymus (Euonymus) leaf in a yellow and white colour scheme. Directly below the spring wreath is a summer circlet, which would also be ideal for a bride. Here I used white gladiolus (Gladiolus), lacey gypsophila (Gypsophila), euphorbia (Euphorbia) and florets of white delphinium (Delphinium) for decoration. To the right of the summer or bridal circlet is an autumnal wreath made of crab apples (Malus), poppy (Papaver) seedheads, black-berries (Rubus fruiticosus), rosehips (Rosa) and florets of hydrangea (Hydrangea macrophylla) heads. And there is also an idea for a winter wreath using ivy (Hedera), rosehips (Rosa), holly (Ilex), berries and lichen twigs. These wreaths can be laid flat on a table or else worn as a head garland. Remember that if you use flowers which are in season and build plenty of foliage into your arrangements you will substantially lower the cost of your materials, although a special celebration may warrant blooms which are a little more than day-to-day.

Annual festivals provide us with the perfect excuse for decorating our surroundings with flowers and foliage. During the Christmas season most people follow the age-old tradition, started during Roman times, of bringing plant material indoors.

In northern climes cut flowers can be in short supply and consequently they are more expensive to buy than during the summer months, so it is an ideal opportunity to make use of different varieties of foliage and berried plants. I draw on all sorts of greenery for Yuletide arrangements, including blue pine *(Pinus)*, rosemary *(Rosmarinus officinalis)*, box *(Buxus)*, yew *(Taxus baccata)*, eucalyptus *(Eucalyptus)*, holly *(Ilex)*, rhododendron *(Rhododendron)*, laurel *(Laurelia)*, bay *(Laurus)* and cypress *(Cupressus)*.

If you want to make a Christmas garland you can either follow the step-by-step method which is illustrated on pages 136–7 or, if you have limited time, you can wire lengths of ivy *(Hedera)* trails together so that they form a long leafy swag and then attach pine cones to the garland. Unless you have access to ivy growing outdoors, which it often does in abundance on walls and tree trunks, I suggest that you buy ivy in potted plant form and cut off the trails for arranging. A wreath is another popular item for marking a festival and a ring of Christmas holly is commonly seen as a symbol of good fortune. There are various different methods of making a circular wreath base.

First, you can purchase a wire frame and pad it with moss; then bind the moss into the frame with florist's reel wire (see the first steps of the Halloween wreath illustrated on page 132). Second, you can use a ready-made florist's foam ring. (If you choose to construct a moss wreath then you should water it at intervals in order to prolong the life of the greenery; the foam ring, once soaked in water, will fulfill the same function.) Third, you can use a twig base: these are available from flower shops, or else you can obtain long, thin and pliable twigs – birch *(Betula)* for example is particularly suitable. Soak the twigs in water to increase their flexibility and then bend them into a circle and bind them with reel wire.

Whatever kind of wreath base you decide to make, once it is ready to decorate group foliage, berries, individual flower heads, fruits and nuts and wire them following the techniques illustrated on pages 174–5 before inserting them directly into the base. A wreath is always eye-catching and welcoming and can be placed in the middle of a table and enhanced with candles or else hung on a vertical surface such as a wall or a front door.

A celebratory meal is an important part of the Christmas festival and so I always like to decorate the table. My favourite blooms at this time of year are combinations of red, cream and green. For example I often use 'Nicole' roses *(Rosa 'Nicole')*, 'Vicki Brown' roses *(Rosa 'Vicki Brown')*, hellebores *(Helleborus)*, also appropriately known as Christmas roses, and fluffy scarlet plume *(Euphorbia fulgens)*.

No Christmas celebration is complete without a bunch of mistletoe *(Viscum album)*,

Festivals

Left: A wreath can be decorated in many ways to suit all kinds of festivals and then hung on a door or placed on a table. Here I covered a mossy base with fresh blue pine (Pinus) before adding various orange fruits, fresh vegetables and bunches of large, dried cinnamon sticks and dried lotus (Nelumbo) seedheads. I used gold spray paint to give sea shells and snails' shells a festive feel. The little green gift boxes are made in Thailand from large tropical leaves.

and the old custom of kissing underneath this romantic plant which, according to myth is a fertility charm, comes from the strange fact that the plant bears fruit in the depths of winter. As an alternative to mistletoe the old-fashioned kissing bough, which sadly seems to have died out, can be made in the same way as the base of a garland. It is shaped like a double hoop and was traditionally decorated with coloured paper and red apples. Once the bough is complete, insert candles and light them ceremoniously for the first time on Christmas Eve and thereafter on each of the twelve days of Christmas. If you

decorate with paper or any other flammable materials (in particular dried plant material) and candles you should never leave the display unattended. Another idea is to construct a German Advent ring – which is an evergreen wreath decorated with pine cones – and add four candles to be lit one by one to mark each Sunday in Advent as Christmas draws near. And of course, there is the universal Christmas tree, which can be embellished with all manner of items from ribbons to colourful fruits and spray-painted dried plant materials.

Once Yuletide is over and the year reaches its close I like to welcome in the New Year with a fresh array of flowers. There are all sorts of possibilities for celebrating the start of a new year with bright, welcoming blooms. For instance, the rich magentas and the serene whites in my mantel shelf arrangement on pages 124–5 will certainly lift the spirits.

Just as candles add a special touch to Christmas and New Year arrangements, so they greatly enhance the impact of flowers when Easter is celebrated. This principal festival of the Christian year ties in with the arrival of spring in the northern hemisphere and at this time of year white and yellow or golden blooms are an appropriate choice and are generally widely available. For a large-scale pedestal arrangement in a church you can use lovely Easter lilies *(Lilium longiflorum)* or any variety of pale chrysanthemums *(Chrysanthemum)*, lacey dill *(Anethum graveolens)*, bushy golden rod *(Solidago)* and vivid green lady's mantle *(Alchemilla mollis)*. However, if you want to create a small-scale display for the home then there are a host of lovely yellow blooms available, such as marigolds *(Calendula)*, gerberas *(Gerbera)* and ranunculus *(Ranunculus)*. Easter is also a good time of year to make a Pot-et-Fleur arrangement, in other words, a display which contains a mixture of planted bulbs such as daffodils *(Narcissus)*, irises *(Iris)*, primulas *(Polianthus)* or cyclamen *(Cyclamen)* and cut flowers which complement your chosen colour scheme (see my arrangement on page 129).

While yellows, creams and whites are particularly suitable for Easter arrangements, darker hues of oranges, russets, reds, golds and browns are ideal for autumnal festivals such as Harvest Festival and Thanksgiving, as well as for Halloween displays. Harvest Festivals offer church flower arrangers wonderful possibilities to work with edible themes. I like to mix dried seedheads with all sorts of fruits and vegetables and thick sheaves of grains and grasses, arranged lavishly around a beautiful loaf of everlasting varnished bread.

NEW YEAR DISPLAY

1 *The ingredients for this New Year arrangement are illustrated on the opposite page.*

Because this is a large-scale display I suggest that you make it in situ. It is designed to sit above a fireplace or on a side table, to be viewed from the front and sides only; the back of the display should be against a wall. First make the base: place a block of wet florist's foam inside a shallow, plastic or waterproof dish. Secure the foam to the dish with waterproof florist's tape. I advise you to fix the dish and the foam to the surface it is resting on with florist's tape – this will help to hold the display firmly in place.

Next take three thick candles of varying heights. (I like to use beeswax candles as they smell delicious. Nevertheless, these are expensive to buy and sadly burn down very quickly. However, if you leave them to chill in a fridge they will burn considerably more slowly.) To wedge the candles into the foam base take lengths of heavy-gauge stub wire and bend each one into a U-shape. Place the U-end against the candle, approximately 1in (2.5cm) above its base. Secure it tightly by winding strong adhesive tape tightly around the bottom of the candle and the top of the U-end several times. Repeat this so that each candle has four large hairpins attached to its base; insert the long prongs of wire directly into the foam.

Flowers
Snow-on-the-mountain (*Euphorbia marginata*)
Euphorbia (*Euphorbia fulgens*)
'Casablanca' lily (*Lilium* 'Casablanca')
Snapdragon (*Antirrhinum*)
'Negretta' tulip (*Tulipa* 'Negretta')
Phalaenopsis orchid (*Phalaenopsis*)
'Madame Pompadour' Singapore orchid
(*Dendrobium* 'Madame Pompadour')
'Karl Rosenfeld' Peony (*Paeonia*
'Karl Rosenfeld')
Lilac (*Syringa*)
Foliage
Ornamental cabbage (*Brassica oleracea*)
Broom (*Genista*)
Ivy (*Hedera*)
Box holly (*Ilex crenata*)
Laurustinus (*Viburnum tinus*)
Bear grass (*Dasylirion*)
Eucalyptus pods (*Eucalyptus*)
Lichen twigs

2 *Begin to add the longest stems of foliage. Insert stems of box holly and strands of bear grass. The bear grass should be bunched together as single*

strands will not be visible from a distance; bind them with reel wire at one end and insert the bound ends directly into the foam. Add sprigs of purple-headed laurustinus and a few trails of ivy. Make sure that the foliage radiates evenly around the foam base.

3 *Add more foliage, beginning with the lichen twigs. Build up the density evenly, making sure that the stems radiate outward from the base of the candles. It is important to place the heavier stems toward the back of the foam base, nearest the wall. If the arrangement is too weighty at the front it may topple forward. Add the snow-on-the-mountain, euphorbia and then stems of lilac and broom.*

4 *Strip the lower leaves off the stems of the ornamental cabbages so that just the frilly hearts are left. Cut the stems short and firmly insert two heavy-gauge stub wires directly into the ends of the stem to lengthen them; add these to the foam base around the bottom of the candles.*

Arrange the purple snapdragons and some single tulips, leaving the leaf on the stems of the tulips. Add the Singapore orchids, the Phalaenopsis orchids and some eucalyptus pods.

Finally, position a few heads of 'Casablanca' lilies as the focal flowers. Infill any gaps and light the candles. The finished New Year display is illustrated on the following page.

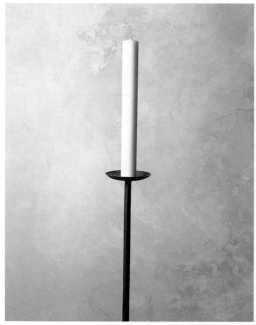
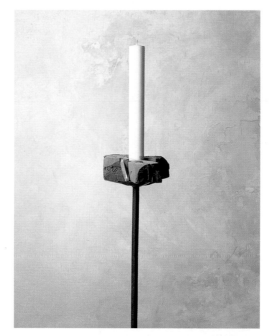

EASTER CANDLE

1 *First condition your flowers, leaving them to stand in nutrient-enriched water for several hours. It is important to give the cut stems a good drink prior to arranging, as once inserted into the florist's foam the stems cannot take up water freely. Meanwhile, take a large Easter candle and secure it to the "spike" of a pedestal candle stand. Make sure that the candle is secure.*

2 *Using strong waterproof florist's tape, secure blocks of wet florist's foam around the base of the candle. Tape each block individually before taping two blocks together. Round off the square edges of each block with a sharp knife, as this makes it much easier to insert the stems.*

3 *Establish an outline with the longer-stemmed foliage: the willow, rosemary and ivy, allowing them to fall loosely and evenly around the candle. If the*

Flowers
Lisianthus (*Eustoma grandiflorum*)
Tuberose (*Polianthes tuberosa*)
'Casablanca' lily (*Lilium* 'Casablanca')
Foliage
Tortured willow (*Salix matsudana* 'Tortuosa')
Butcher's broom (*Ruscus*)
Guelder rose (*Viburnum opulus*)
Viburnum (*Viburnum laurestinus*)
Rosemary (*Rosmarinus officinalis*)
Ivy (*Hedera*)

candle is to be viewed from all angles, you must make sure that the plant material is evenly spread all around the pedestal; if on the other hand it is to stand against a

wall then you need only arrange plant material three-quarters of the way around the base.

4 *Next add your flowering foliage: the guelder rose, viburnum and butcher's broom and cut the stems to appropriate lengths in order to create a well-balanced display. Use as much foliage as you wish to achieve the required density.*

5 *Now add the cut flower stems – the lisianthus and tuberoses. This Easter arrangement is appropriately formal because of its limited colour scheme of green and white. Make sure that there are no gaps in the arrangement and that none of the florist's foam is visible through the display. Infill any gaps with remaining plant material.*

6 *The final touch is to add the 'Casablanca' lily heads to draw the eye and act as the focal flowers. The finished Easter Candle is illustrated opposite.*

P O T - E T - F L E U R

1 *Assemble the materials. Take an old metal bucket and place two galvanized or watertight containers inside it (these will hold the stems of the cut flowers). Wedge the two containers firmly into the bucket with old crocks and then cover the crocks with soil and peat moss. If you do not wish to scratch the metal buckets or the containers then line the outer container with a piece of heavy plastic sheeting – this will also help in the final cleaning-up process.*

2 *Remove the pots from all the potted plants. Start by placing the tallest plants – the amaryllis and the Easter lilies – into the soil. Top up the soil or peat moss if necessary so that the roots are covered. This arrangement is designed to be seen from the front only, so place the tallest stems around one half of the bucket, leaving space in front for shorter plant material to stand.*

Potted flowers
Amaryllis (Hippeastrum)
Jasmine (Jasminum)
'Pansy' orchid (Miltoniopsis)
Gardenia (Gardenia)
Easter lily (Lilium longiflorum)
Cut flowers
Bells of Ireland (Moluccella laevis)
Onion heads (Allium aflatunense)
Arum lily (Zantedeschia)
Euphorbia (Euphorbia fulgens)
Painter's palette (Anthurium)

3 *Fill the two inner containers with water. Add the rest of the potted plants – the orchids, the gardenia*

and the jasmine – to the soil, making sure that their roots are well-covered by soil or peat moss and that the blooms and foliage are not crushed and fall loosely over the rim of the bucket.

4 *Add the cut stems to the two containers holding the water, placing the tallest stems – the moluccella (also known sometimes as bells of Ireland) and the onion heads – behind the shorter arum lilies. Build up an even density of plant material, infilling any gaps in the Pot-et-Fleur. Arrange the painter's palettes over the rim of the bucket and trail the euphorbia and more jasmine toward the front, so that the display does not look too formal. If you line the bucket, make sure that you trim away any visible plastic. The finished Pot-et-Fleur is illustrated on the opposite page. This is a scented arrangement and is ideal for an Easter or springtime celebration.*

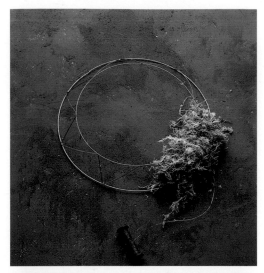

HALLOWEEN WREATH

1 *Assemble the materials (these are illustrated on the previous page). Buy a copper wire base from a florist, or make your own from a coathanger. This is done by bending a length of stiff wire into a circle and fastening the ends with reel wire. Repeat the process to make a smaller circle of wire. The smaller circle forms the upper layer of the base, and the larger circle the lower layer. Position the two circles at least 2in (5cm) apart and wire them together in a zigzag pattern as shown in the picture. Start to cover the base with the moss. As you add the moss to the base, wind reel wire tightly around it to secure it to the frame of the wreath.*

2 *When you have finished covering the base and have bound the moss padding tightly with reel wire, make a wire loop on the larger circle of the frame so that you can hang the finished wreath.*

3 *Make groups or bunches of beech and berried ivy and wire the stems with double-leg mount wire (see Techniques, pages 176-7). If you bunch the foliage together it will have more impact than if you use individual sprigs. Then wire the pomegranates individually and add them to the base. To secure the wired group of foliage to the wreath, insert the wire at an angle opposite to the way you in fact want to*

Flowers
Ice plant *(Sedum spectabile)*
Oriental poppy *(Papaver orientale)*
Hydrangea *(Hydrangea macrophylla)*
Chinese lantern *(Physalis)*

Foliage
Berried ivy *(Hedera helix)*
Cotoneaster *(Cotoneaster conspicuus)*
'Autumn' eucalyptus
(Eucalyptus sturtiana)
Beech *(Fagus sylvatica)*
Lichen *(Peltigera canina)*
Honesty *(Lunaria)*
Golden rod *(Solidago)*
Teasel *(Dipsacus fullonum)*
Moss

Fruits
Blackberry *(Rubus fruiticosus)*
Gourd *(Cucurbita)*
Date *(Phoenix dactylifera)*
Walnut *(Juglans regia)*
Chestnut *(Castanea sativa)*
Cobnut *(Corylus avellana)*
Pomegranate *(Punica granatum)*
Rosehip *(Rosa eglanteria)*

position it. Once the wire is fully inserted into the wreath, bend the foliage attached to it in the opposite direction to anchor it firmly.

4 *Add the lichen twigs in-between the leaves – cut the stems to a length of about 4in (10cm) and then push them gently into the wreath, so that they do not snap. Curl the flexible young date stems into a loop and wire them into the base.*

5 *Add textural contrast by inserting a few wired teasels in front of the pomegranates, and feed the golden rod in-between the beech leaves and the lichen twigs. Next, add red-berried cotoneaster sprays and sprigs of honesty.*

6 *Working forward from the teasels insert wired groups of eucalyptus leaves, blackberries, rosehips and ice plant. Individually wire and insert the gourds, walnuts, Chinese lanterns and poppy seedheads and spear in a few immature green date stems. Cut the stems of the hydrangeas short and double-leg mount wire them (see Techniques, pages 176-7). Then insert them into the base. Use your scissors to tidy up any stray stems. Swivel the wreath as you work and fill in any gaps with red berries, rosehips and beech leaves. The finished Halloween Wreath is illustrated opposite.*

Halloween is a popular festival which is celebrated on both sides of the Atlantic, but the autumnal or fall festival of Thanksgiving is traditional to North America. Both these special events are ideal occasions to decorate your surroundings, or perhaps create a gift arrangement with seasonal vegetables, flowers and foliage.

Halloween falls on October 31 on the eve of All Saints' Day and derives its name from All Hallows (or 'holy') Eve. In pre-Christian times it was commonly believed that on the last night in October the souls of the dead revisited their homes, and even after All Saints' Day became a recognized Christian festival the supernatural associations of All Hallows survived. Centuries ago it was customary to carve demon faces in the hard outer skins of vegetables such as pumpkins *(Cucurbita maxima)*, turnips *(Brassica rapa)* or swedes *(Brassica napus)* in order to ward off evil spirits associated with All Hallows, and the practice of making ghoulish "Jack-o'-lanterns" – the hallmarks of Halloween – by hollowing out squashes and placing a candle inside them continues to the present day.

The date of Thanksgiving varies from year to year. It was originally observed by the Pilgrim Fathers who formally celebrated their first harvest in 1621 on the fourth Thursday in November. Since 1863 this day has been a national holiday in the United States and an occasion to look back and give thanks for the blessings of the year gone by. However, in Canada Thanksgiving is celebrated on the second Monday in October. If you observe this festival then it is traditional to share a special family meal and also to eat pumpkin pie, so why not decorate the table with seasonal plant material to celebrate this special day?

In northern climes, when Halloween, Thanksgiving or Guy Fawkes Night (which falls on 5 November) come around annually there are all sorts of autumnal or fall ingredients available in warm shades of yellow, orange, red, russet and brown. This is a perfect time of the year to construct a wreath or a welcome ring to hang on the door, perhaps for a fireworks party, a Harvest supper or a Thanksgiving reunion. Wreath-making also offers an ideal opportunity to involve children in flower arranging. Collecting raw materials is as much part of the fun as arranging them, and preparing the ingredients is an activity which children can participate in, learn from and enjoy. You can garner all sorts of decorative organic materials on country walks or from the garden and hedgerows, or, if you live in an urban area with no access to plant material growing wild then you can purchase seedheads, teasels, twigs and red berries such as spindle *(Euonymus europaeus)*, sweet briar *(Rosa eglanteria)* and firethorn *(Pyracantha coccinea)* from florists or flower markets.

Other decorative ingredients I often use to make wreaths and welcome rings include: pomegranates *(Punica granatum)*, rosehips *(Rosa)*, crab apples *(Malus)*, ornamental peppers *(Capsicum frutescens)*, honesty *(Lunaria)*, Chinese lanterns *(Physalis)*, woolly old man's beard *(Clematis)*, leaves such as copper beech *(Fagus sylvatica)*, grasses, all sorts of herbs and fern or bracken. It is important to gather your materials before the first frosts of winter arrive and also before the birds have taken their pickings! One of the advantages of wreaths is that you can leave them to dessicate so that they make attractive long-lasting dried arrangements.

For Halloween or for a family Thanksgiving celebration, instead of making a traditional Jack-'o-lantern by carving a devilish face in a pumpkin (Cucurbita maxima) and illumi-nating it with a lighted candle, try adapting the pumpkin theme as I have opposite. I cut holes in the skin of a large pumpkin and blocked them with wet florist's foam for inserting the stems. My decorative plant material includes lichen twigs, oriental bittersweet (Celastrus orbiculatus), contorted poppy (Papaver) seedheads, smoke bush (Cotinus), immature dates (Phoenix dactylifera), gourds (Cucurbita), Chinese lanterns (Physalis), maize (Zea mays) seedheads and Caucasian oak leaves (Quercus macranthera).

CHRISTMAS GARLAND

1 *On the opposite page the ingredients of my Christmas garland are illustrated – any or all of these make suitable Christmas decoration. This garland is large and heavy – so make sure that you have a large, flat surface to work on. Cut sprigs of foliage to roughly the same length; group approximately five sprigs and bind them tightly together with medium-gauge stub wire using the double leg-mount technique (see page 176-7).*

2 *Take bound sprigs of rosemary, holly, viburnum berries, skimmia and pine spruce and bind them tightly into a bunch with reel wire.*

3 *When you have wired numerous bunches in this way, bind them together with reel wire so that the garland begins to take shape. All the plant material must point in the same direction.*

4 *Build up the garland by adding further bunches of foliage, securing them as you work with reel wire. The first half of the garland should measure approximately 4ft (1m).*

5 *Repeat steps 1 to 4 in order to make the second half of the garland. Again, all the bunches should point in the same direction. Join the two halves firmly together with reel wire.*

Start to prepare additional decorative elements to add to the garland. Take three orchids and wire them together; bind and tie stems of lemon grass and

Flowers
Hanging amaranthus *(Amaranthus caudatus)*
'Charmeur' carnation *(Dianthus 'Charmeur')*
'Baccarolla' rose *(Rosa 'Baccarolla')*
Red Singapore orchid *(Orchid arnthera)*
Kangaroo paw *(Anigozanthos)*
Christmas rose *(Helleborus)*
Flowering skimmia *(Skimmia)*
Dried lotus seedhead *(Nelumbo)*
Sea holly *(Eryngium)*

Foliage
Berried holly *(Ilex aquifolium)*
Blue pine spruce *(Picea)*
Blue-berried viburnum *(Viburnum)*
Willow *(Salix matsudana 'Tortuosa')*
Snake grass *(Scirpus tabernaemontani)*
Box *(Buxus)*
Sorbus berries *(Sorbus)*
Rosemary *(Rosmarinus officinalis)*
Lemon grass *(Cymbopogon citratus)*

Fruits, vegetables and spices
Cinnamon sticks *(Cinnamomum zeylanicum)*
Miniature aubergine *(Solanum)*
Apple *(Malus domestica)*
Walnuts *(Juglans)*
Whole garlic cloves *(Allium sativum)*
Radish *(Raphanus sativus)*

sticks of cinnamon into bundles; wire cloves of garlic, radishes and miniature aubergines (see Techniques, page 176). Prepare two small terra-cotta pots which will make a pair of "bells" – insert a heavy-gauge stub wire through the hole in the base and then spiral the end of the wire inside the pot so that it cannot slip out through the hole. Wire two walnuts (see Techniques, page 176) and insert the wire through the hole in the base of the pot.

Next group a few stems of kangaroo paw together and individually wire the flower heads of carnations, Christmas roses (these are also known as hellebores) and 'Baccarolla' roses. Bunch together some tassels of velvety hanging amaranthus. Then wire dried lotus seedheads, sea holly and some red apples. You can embellish the garland with any decoration you like, for instance: peppers, fresh green peppercorns, bark-covered balls and grapes. Add the terra-cotta bells to the middle of the garland and attach a bow made of wide taffeta ribbon (see Techniques, pages 178-9). When you have finished decorating the garland you can hang it on a mantel shelf using tacks or high-tension wire – it is weighty and should be well supported. Florist's tape will help to hold the garland in place and will leave no marks. The finished Christmas Garland is illustrated on the following page.

For many people, a wedding is a major occasion for family and friends where flowers are a prominent and often a costly part of the ceremony, whatever form it may take. Although christenings, anniversaries and other types of festivals throughout the year are undoubtedly enhanced by floral decoration, the importance attached to weddings of all kinds of religious faiths singles out a marriage ceremony as one of the most special events of a lifetime. With a little forethought and planning you can choose flowers and foliage which will add a personal note to a wedding day and also perhaps reflect the spiritual as well as the celebratory aspects of the important event.

For the knowledgable flower enthusiast a wedding day can be an opportunity where ideas and creativity come to the fore. But for those who know little about the enormous variety of blooms and foliage on offer, the occasion may well seem daunting. Whatever your experience with planning flowers for embellishing an important occasion, relevant books and magazines provide all sorts of inspiration.

Most brides sensibly opt to rely on the assistance of a trained florist who will be able to offer advice and ideas. And although friends or acquaintances who are practised flower arrangers may provide a valuable contribution, I usually advise brides to leave intricate bridal work to someone skilled as the delicate wiring involved is very time-consuming. Some of the techniques for bridal work explained in this book are those I use in my work, but this area of floristry certainly requires practice.

Smaller wedding flower items are easily and conveniently made by friends or relatives and will help to cut down the overall expense. For instance, buttonholes and corsages are not difficult to construct. All that is required are some blooms in prime condition – for instance lovely white or cream rosebuds which are just beginning to open. You can pin the sepals to neaten the flower head with small U-shaped pins (see Techniques, pages 172-3). For each buttonhole, cut the stem short and add an ivy (Hedera) leaf, a spray of fern (Asparagus) or a few berries and then bind the two together with green florist's tape. Headdresses – in the form of circlets, crowns and combs decorated with small flowers, the florets of larger blooms and leaves – are quite simple to prepare and make delightful additions to wedding attire. On the left-hand side of page 116 there are two pretty bridal garlands which can be worn on the head. You should use colours and blooms which complement the bride's bouquet or tied bunch and you should wire the flowers or florets from,

for example, delphiniums *(Delphinium)* to make the headdress look delicate and feel light to wear. I also enjoy constructing arrangements for the bridesmaids or page boys to carry – for example, small basketfuls of blooms, hoops made from natural twigs laced with flowers and pomanders hanging from a hand-held ribbon.

Once you have decided on the date of the wedding – in northern climes the summer months are particularly popular and at this time of year flowers are in abundance which is an

Weddings

Left: A hanging ball of flowers for a wedding reception. First I filled two semi-spherical hanging baskets with wet florist's foam and joined them together with heavy-gauge wire. Next I hung the ball in position and then began arranging. I used spires of Foxtail lilies (Eremurus), delphiniums (Delphinium), stocks (Matthiola) and 'Doris Rijke' spray roses (Rosa 'Doris Rijke'). Use large-leafed varieties to save on costly flowers and give density.

advantage for the buyer – you can begin to ascertain what varieties will be available. In the main, it is sensible to choose flowers which are in season as out-of-season varieties are not only costly but are rarely robust. The next thing to consider is what the colour theme for the day will be: the bride's dress and the clothes worn by the bridesmaids and page boys and any other attendants will to some extent dictate the flowers you choose. Today all sorts of colour themes are acceptable at weddings, from traditional white or cream to predominantly pink, apricot or yellow themes and even bolder

statements made with strong-hued reds, purples and blues. Once you have chosen your colour theme and decided whether you wish to have a traditional wedding or something more unusual then you can begin to select your flowers accordingly.

The blooms which will receive particular attention on a wedding day will be the bride's bouquet. In the early decades of the 20th century brides carried massive shower bouquets which trailed from the waist to the ground. These were usually made of gardenias *(Gardenia)* and lilies *(Lilium)* mixed with ferns and herbs and twined into "love knots". By the 1920s and 1930s bouquets were less extravagant and small-scale posies became popular – they were often made with scented flowers such as mock orange *(Philadelphus)* and lily-of-the-valley *(Convallaria majalis)*. By the 1970s large-scale flowing bouquets were once again in vogue and for the last 20 years both labour-intensive wired bouquets and natural tied bunches with plenty of foliage have been in great demand.

The bride's choice of flowers will to some extent dictate what shape, size and structure the bouquet will take. Small and delicate flowers and foliage will generally have to be wired and "sprayed" together in order to have some visual impact. The advantage of wiring is that the bouquet will look light and delicate and will remain intact if, for example, it is a windy day. However, wiring is a lengthy process and adds to the expense of the bouquet as it may take even a trained florist up to half a day to complete a wired bouquet. For this reason I often suggest a tied bunch falling in a shower or else held over the arm, or perhaps a posy – these are much quicker and simpler to make and look more natural and attractive. Church weddings offer all sorts of possibilities for decorating with flowers, from imposing pedestal arrangements to small-scale trailing pew-end embellishments. Although special pew-end bases are now available (see Techniques, pages 172-3) it is as effective and almost simpler to make a tied swag or bunch instead and secure it to the end of the pew end with a ribbon. You can also decorate the altar, window sills, hanging lights, arches, the pulpit and the font.

For Jewish weddings I am often asked to decorate the chuppah or cover under which the wedding ceremony must take place. Some of my favourite chuppahs are out of doors in a garden setting where poles entwined with foliage and flowers support a white canopy draped with fragrant jasmine *(Jasminum)* and wax flowers *(Stephanotis)*.

RED BRIDAL BOUQUET

1 *Assemble the flowers (see the previous page). Strip away the lower leaves from the stems and de-thorn the roses using a sharp knife. Singe the ends of the euphorbia stems (see Techniques, page 174). Only the lilies and the berries are wired in this bouquet (see Techniques, pages 176-7). Arrange the foliage on a flat surface in the shape you require the bouquet to take.*

2 *Bind the stem ends together with string – this will be the handle of the bouquet.*

3 *Arrange the euphorbia, Singapore orchids and roses over the foliage base. Place the longest-stemmed flowers in the middle, reserving the shorter*

Flowers
Arum lily *(Zantedeschia aethiopica)*
Red Singapore orchid *(Orchid arnthera)*
'Baccarolla' rose *(Rosa 'Baccarolla')*
Scarlet plume *(Euphorbia fulgens)*
'Fragrant Cloud' rose *(Rosa 'Fragrant Cloud')*
'Yellow Ribbon' lily *(Lilium 'Yellow Ribbon')*

Foliage
Beech *(Fagus sylvatica)*
Grevillea *(Grevillea)*
Snowberry *(Symphoricarpos albus)*
Guelder rose *(Viburnum opulus)*
Butcher's broom *(Ruscus asculeatus)*

stems for the periphery of the bouquet. Bind the ends of all the stems and also the wired lilies and berries securely together with string.

4 *Add the arum lilies, the dark 'Baccarolla' roses and the viburnum berries. You should graduate the density of the bouquet so that the outer edges are thinner than the middle. Finally, take the wired heads of the 'Yellow Ribbon' lilies and secure them with reel wire into the middle of the bouquet. The finished Red Bridal Bouquet is illustrated opposite. Bind all the wires and stem ends once again with string, then cover the string with a ribbon, tying a bow (see Techniques, pages 178-9).*

SHOWER BOUQUET

1 *First condition all the cut flowers. Once they are made up into the bouquet they will not be able to drink, so it is important to give them plenty of water to drink before you start arranging.*

Most wedding bouquets are wired – this holds the flowers in place and also reduces the weight of the bouquet considerably so that the bride can hold it comfortably. The secret behind making a traditional shower bouquet is to strip away the stems of your chosen flowers and foliage and wire each one individually. A variety of wiring techniques are illustrated on pages 176-7. You should cover the silver wires with green tape to create a more natural effect (see Techniques, page 177). The foliage forms the base of the bouquet: lay the wired greenery into the required shape and join all the exposed wire ends together; bend them at a right angle to form the handle of the bouquet.

After establishing the foliage base, start to wire the individual flower heads. Use a light-gauge wire which allows the flowers some movement – the blooms should not be too rigidly wired, otherwise the bouquet will look stiff and unnatural. However, the heavier flower heads such as the lilac, peonies and

Flowers
Delphinium *(Delphinium)*
'Longi' lily *(Lilium longiflorium)*
'Tineke' rose *(Rosa 'Tineke')*
"Mme Florent Stepman' lilac
(Syringa 'Mme Florent Stepman')
Stephanotis *(Stephanotis floribunda)*
Sweet pea *(Lathyrus odoratus)*
'Casablanca' lily *(Lilium 'Casablanca')*
Peony *(Paeonia)*

Foliage
Ivy *(Hedera)*
Mock orange *(Philadelplus coronarius)*
Bear grass *(Dasylirion)*

'Casablanca' lilies need a medium-gauge wire in order to provide sufficient support.

2 *Bind the wires forming the handle tightly together with reel wire. Add the wired 'Trumpet' lilies to the leaf base, securing them with reel wire. Then add the smaller flowers and continue to build up the desired shape of the bouquet, making sure*

that all the faces of the flowers are pointing forward. As you position each individual flower make sure that it is secured with reel wire to the main body of the bouquet. I advise removing the stamens from the lilies with a pair of scissors as these tend to stain the petals and could ruin the bride's dress.

3 *As you construct the bouquet it will become heavier. It is useful to have a stable, heavy-based pot or vase to hand: place the handle of the bouquet inside the container, and drape the plant material over the rim. It helps to make the bouquet in front of a mirror so that you can see how it looks as you work and spot any gaps.*

4 *Make sure that the bouquet has an even density of flowers and foliage all around. Finally, add the 'Casablanca' lilies as the focal flowers, securing them with reel wire. Trim any protruding wires with scissors and tightly bind the wires forming the bouquet handle with reel wire. Cover the handle with green tape. The final touch is to spiral a white ribbon up and down the handle several times, making sure that all the tape and wire are concealed; tie a bow at the top of the handle. The finished Shower Bouquet is illustrated opposite.*

One of the most charming ways you can choose to acknowledge an anniversary, whether it is the arrival of a new-born child, a coming of age birthday celebration, a wedding anniversary or a remembrance to a departed loved one, is to do so with flowers.

If you wish to send someone flowers for an anniversary and order them through a florist then it is always a good idea to stipulate exactly which blooms and what kind of display you require. More traditional florists tend to relay flat, cellophane-covered bouquets, whereas others specialize in the European style of presenting flowers, the tied bunch (see page 175). The advantage of sending a tied bunch is that when it reaches the recipient no arranging is necessary and it can simply be put directly into a vase.

Birthdays in general are perfect occasions for giving flowers and also for decorating surroundings with plant material for a party. If you are planning a celebration then there are various factors to take into consideration. For instance, if you are holding a party inside a marquee then the colour of the lining should complement the flowers, or, if you plan to have a summer garden party out of doors then you can erect sun shades and decorate the central supporting pole with flowers and trailing ivy *(Hedera)*. I have also had the pleasure of arranging the flowers for a winter celebration where I strung chains of fairy lights over potted greenery and banks of white hydrangeas *(Hydrangea macrophylla)* to give the idea of a snowy scene.

Whatever the age of the person celebrating a birthday all sorts of fun themes are possible, and birthdays are special occasions when you can be daring and inventive. You should consider the age of the person in question and any favourite colours and varieties of flowers they may have. By using chicken or mesh wire and reel wire you can mould moss into all sorts of shapes. For instance, for someone who likes cats you can construct a cat from moss and wire and decorate it with flowers to add a personal note to your gift. Coming of age birthdays and the more significant milestones such as fortieth or fiftieth birthdays call for something memorable and you can make a special display using a few flamboyant flowers. If you have a restricted budget you should go to a wholesale source such as a local flower market; although you generally have to buy in bulk you will find a wide selection of blooms at competitive prices.

Perhaps you could create an Eastern theme for a birthday party using a few striking orchids

and lots of potted palms and maybe embellish the table with fresh green bamboo, tropical fruits and flowers (see Tropical themes, page 42). I am most grateful to a client who asked me to construct a coming of age arrangement combining tropical flowers with water and candles – the result is illustrated on page 153. Whether floating on water or fixed into a candle cup, candles are especially useful ingredients for making anniversary arrangements. Bobbing on water, their soft flames are reflected which

Anniversaries

Left: A hanging candelabra decorated with flowers and beeswax candles would make an ideal accompaniment for a special anniversary celebration. I secured wet florist's foam around the candle cups with tape and added masterwort (Astrantia), pale 'Porcelain' roses (Rosa 'Porcelina'), dark 'Baccarolla' roses (Rosa 'Baccarolla'), 'Imperial Gold' lilies (Lilium 'Imperial Gold'), pink achillea (Achillea), love-in-a-mist seedheads (Nigella damascena) and ivy (Hedera).

accentuates the gentle and friendly ambience they create. Flower arrangements incorporating candles are also suitable for parties held out of doors or in marquees where electric lighting may not be available, and, if enough are used, they also provide adequate lighting for an after-dark occasion. I particularly like to use candles when making wedding anniversary arrangements as they add a touch of romance. Because flowers arranged around a candle stick or a candelabra are raised above table level they have a particularly strong visual impact. You can achieve an effective and inexpensive display

using quite a modest amount of flowers and infilling with plenty of decorative foliage, leaving you all the more to spend on champagne!

I am quite often asked to prepare gifts for anniversaries and it can be useful to remember the various symbols of yearly anniversaries as a starting point. For example, paper is symbolic of the first anniversary, and it is not difficult to decorate flowers with paper wrapping and bows. Also you may be able to find appropriately named blooms such as 'Paper White' daffodils *(Narcissus* 'Paper White') or the attractive variegated foliage known as parchment bark *(Pittosporum tobira* 'Variegatum'). Cotton marks the second anniversary and also offers scope to the arranger, for instance, my arrangement of dried twigs covered with fluffy white balls of cotton on page 60, or pretty cotton grass *(Eriophorum)* or lavender cotton *(Santolina chamaecyparissus)*, which has aromatic gray foliage and yellow button flowers – this plant dries well and is said to work as an effective moth repellent. For a third anniversary the symbol is leather, so you could make use of leatherleaf *(Chamaedaphne calyculata)* in an arrangement, and the fourth anniversary, which is symbolized with fruit and flowers offers limitless opportunities!

Wedding anniversaries are often celebrated with flowers. It is a delightful idea to remind a spouse of their actual wedding day by choosing flowers which appeared on the day of the marriage. For silver wedding anniversaries, celebrated after 25 years (as well as the rather more unusual diamond anniversaries, celebrated after 60 years of marriage), white blooms are appropriate (see the section on white flowers, on pages 102-9). For ruby anniversaries, celebrated after 40 years, a red colour theme is most suitable (see the section on red flowers on pages 70-5). And for golden anniversaries, celebrated after 50 years, yellows are most appropriate (see the section on yellow blooms on pages 78-85). Whatever the anniversary, there are plenty of apposite varieties you can use: for a silver anniversary 'Little Silver' roses *(Rosa* 'Little Silver')*, which are a pretty pale pink colour, or perhaps 'Silver Cristal' trachelium *(Trachelium aeruleum* 'Silver Cristal'*)* and leaf such as silver birch *(Betula pendula)*. For a ruby anniversary you can choose 'Ruby Red' tulips *(Tulipa* 'Ruby Red'*)* or 'Ruby' roses *(Rosa* 'Ruby'*)*. And for a golden anniversary perhaps 'Golden Apeldoorn' tulips *(Tulipa* 'Golden Apeldoorn'*)* and golden rod *(Solidago)*, to name just a few.

COMING OF AGE

1 *Assemble the materials (see the previous page). First condition the cut flowers by leaving them in nutrient-enriched water for several hours. Meanwhile start to prepare the base of the arrangement. Take some florist's foam and cut it with a sharp knife into a ring. Trim away the square edges of the foam with a knife – this makes it easier to insert stems into the foam. Place a shallow bowl into the middle of the ring.*

2 *Cut the stems of the foliage short and start grouping it with the moss. Bend lengths of stub wire into a hairpin shape and pin the moss and foliage into the ring (see Techniques, page 177).*

3 *Cut the stems of all the flowers (except the birds of paradise and the tortured willow which remain long in order to give the display height), leaving approximately 1in (2.5cm) of stem below the flower head to insert into the ring. Group these flowers together and bind them with wire before*

Flowers
Nutans *(Leucospermum cordifolium)*
'Joyce' gerbera *(Gerbera 'Joyce')*
'Mona Lisa' Anemone *(Anemone 'Mona Lisa')*
Bloodflower *(Haemanthus)*
Trachelium *(Trachelium caeruleum)*
Sea holly *(Eryngium)*
Bird of paradise *(Strelitzia reginae)*

Foliage
Protea *(Protea)*
Red sunset *(Leucadendron)*
Tortured willow *(Salix matsudana 'Tortuosa')*
Bun moss

pinning them firmly into the ring. The flowers will have much more visual impact grouped together than if they are inserted individually.

4 *Fill in any gaps in the ring with the heads of the gerberas and the blue anemones.*

5 *Take a pinholder and press it down firmly on a piece of fixing clay in the middle of the flat base of the bowl. The pinholder must be made secure otherwise the long stems of the central plant material will topple over. Carefully insert the stems of the birds of paradise and the tortured willow into the pins of the pinholder. Do not overcrowd the pinholder, as a few well-positioned stems will have a striking impact. You can strip fresh willow branches if you cannot obtain dried willow. Make sure that the heads of the birds of paradise are all facing outward.*

6 *Fill the bowl with water so that it almost reaches the rim and then add small coloured stones and white pebbles to conceal the pinholder. Float some small bobbing candles on the surface of the water. The final touch is to light the candles. The finished Coming of Age arrangement is illustrated opposite.*

SILVER WEDDING ANNIVERSARY

1 *First assemble your materials. You will need some wet florist's foam, tape and fixing clay as well as candle cups and candle holders (see Techniques, pages 172-3). Leave the cut flowers in nutrient-enriched water for several hours – this will ensure that they last well. Once inserted into the florist's foam it is less easy for the stems to take up water.*

Cut a piece of florist's foam so that it fits snugly inside a candle cup. Trim down the square edges of the foam; this makes it easier to insert the flower stems into the foam. Allow the piece of foam to protrude well above the rim of the candle cup so that the same depth of foam sits above and below the rim. Secure the foam firmly onto the cup using strong, waterproof florist's tape. Then insert the candle cup into the candlestick or candelabra using a ball of florist's fixing clay.

Flowers
Lisianthus *(Eustoma grandiflorum)*
Brodiaea *(Triteleia)*
'Little Silver' rose *(Rosa 'Little Silver')*
'Porcelain' rose *(Rosa 'Porcelina')*
Bluebell *(Hyacinthoides scilla)*
Sweet pea *(Lathyrus odoratus)*
Scabious *(Scabiosa caucasica)*

Foliage
Eucalyptus *(Eucalyptus gunnii)*
'Autumn' eucalyptus
(*Eucalyptus sturtiana*)
Ivy *(Hedera)*

2 *Establish the outline of your arrangement using the stems of eucalyptus and trails of ivy, making sure*

that you use plenty of flowing foliage in order to give the whole display shape and movement. If you have access to a garden collect ivy trails from trees and walls; if you cannot find ready-cut ivy trails, then buy some potted ivy and cut off the trail ends.

3 *Take the brodiaea, roses and bluebells and insert those with the weakest stems first. As you continue to build up the arrangement make sure that it is taking the required shape and that there is an all-round even density of leaf and flowers when the display is viewed from back and front.*

4 *Add the focal flowers – the lisianthus, sweet peas and scabious. Make sure that there are no gaps in the arrangement and that none of the mechanics are visible. Put the candles in place and finally light them. The finished Silver Wedding anniversary arrangement is illustrated on the opposite page.*

As I am so fond of flowers I am always overjoyed when people bring me blooms at home, even though I have a shop full of them! What is interesting about the process of giving flowers is that the giver chooses certain combinations of blooms and foliage which either tend to reflect what plant material they themselves like or what they think the recipient will like, or a mixture of the two.

Because there is such a huge variety of plant material available today and because flowers are so universally popular, with a little thought as to what best suits the recipient (taking into account their colour preferences and their surroundings) the process of giving is as pleasurable as that of receiving. And even if you do perhaps make a wrong choice cut flowers are not ever-lasting, so an error of judgment will only be short-lived! In countries such as the Netherlands, where flowers have long been regarded as one of the great joys of life, both men and women commonly give and receive flowers. Happily, the British misconception that men do not appreciate flowers, seems gradually to be changing and now more and more men seem to be enthusiastic buyers, senders and recipients of cut blooms.

If you send gift flowers via a relay floristry service then be sure to give precise details of which blooms you require, what colour scheme you want and whether you want a traditional bouquet wrapped in cellophane, or a tied bunch or perhaps a display in a basket with a handle to facilitate carrying. If you do not give the relay service these details then it is likely that whoever you are sending flowers to will receive a multi-coloured selection with very little harmony.

However, if you have time to choose, arrange and deliver the flowers yourself then so much the better. I advise careful packing of cut stems if you have to travel some distance in order to transport gift flowers. First, you should make sure that the flower heads are well protected, so wrap the bouquet or bunch in attractive paper or better still cellophane – as this allow the beauty of the flowers to be fully visible. Second, for a long journey it is best to place the stem ends in a bucket of water (make sure that the bucket is no more than half-full otherwise there will be spillages), as this allows the flowers to drink en route; flowers are best transported in an upright position.

As an alternative you can lay flowers carefully in a shallow box, but you must remember that they will need a long drink on arrival at your destination. Although there are many sorts of decorative boxes available, many of these have a "window" made of cellophane which usually

requires the flowers to be cut short, which seems a pity. Whenever you cover flowers with cellophane, whether you present them in a box or as a bouquet, you must remember that plants need to breathe and if confined inside an airless wrapping they will cause condensation: so prick a few small holes in the cellophane to prevent this happening. For more information on how to present flowers see pages 178–9.

When transporting very delicate flowers or specimen stems, for example roses *(Rosa)* or

Gifts

Left: A spiralled bunch makes a pretty, portable gift. I mixed gloriosas (Gloriosa), 'La Minuet' roses (Rosa 'La Minuet'), tree mallow (Lavatera), dahlias (Dahlia), arum lilies (Zantedeschia) and red valerian (Centranthus ruber). After spiralling the stems (see page 175), cut all the ends to an even length and wrap them in cellophane. Tie the bunch with string and cover with an ivy (Hedera) trail and a "tail" of hanging amaranthus (Amaranthus caudatus).

orchids, you may notice that these can be commonly purchased with a small tube filled with a nutrient-enriched solution attached to the end of the stem. You should leave this tube attached until the last moment, as this helps to keep the petals fresh and prevent wilting.

The birth of a baby is a special occasion which is traditionally celebrated with flowers. To mark such an important event it is practical to send the mother and child a pre-arranged tied bunch which can simply be placed into a vase, or perhaps a basket arrangement: if the mother and baby are still in hospital then this will save

the time of busy nursing staff. It is also a good idea to provide a container with the gift as hospitals are so inundated with flowers that consequently they are often short of containers. Or, if you wish to mark the day that a child is born to a close relative or a friend then a small ornamental or flowering tree is a thoughtful idea, and this sort of gift carries appropriate symbolism as a reminder of the "tree of life". If the recipient has a garden then the tree can be planted and should last for many years. For instance, a small rose *(Rosa)* tree or a cherry *(Prunus)* tree would make a wonderful gift for the family to see grow as the child gets older. If the recipient does not have a garden then there are alternatives to this idea, such as a box *(Buxus)* or a bay *(Laurus)* tree – these need not be transplanted outside, but survive happily in a pot. Alternatively you could make a topiary tree using dried plant material, this of course will last for an indefinite period. For small children it is fun to make teddy bears or animals from small-gauge chicken or mesh wire and moss, bound together with reel wire.

Mother's Day, which falls on the fourth Sunday in Lent in Britain and on the second Sunday in May in the United States is a day for remembering mothers and an ideal occasion for giving with flowers. During the last century, when many people worked in service in large households this was the day when they returned home to visit their mothers, traditionally offering posies of violets *(Viola odorata)*. My Mother's Day posy is illustrated on pages 164–5.

If you know people who are interested in astrology then you can obtain astrology charts which are compiled by the British Flowers and Plants Association and choose certain varieties and colours relating to star signs – this is a novel way of putting together gift blooms and foliage. Another idea is to give a long-lasting gift to someone who has a garden. For instance, you can buy seeds or unopened bulbs of tulips *(Tulipa)*, hyacinths *(Hyacinthus)* or daffodils *(Narcissus)* and present them together with some cut stems of the same variety – the blooms will give a foretaste of the beauty locked up inside the accompanying seeds or bulbs.

Wreaths also make delightful gifts. On page 117 there is a mid-summer's circlet of delphinium *(Delphinium)* florets, asters *(Aster)*, lady's mantle *(Alchemilla mollis)* and marguerite daisies *(Chrysanthemum frutescens)*. The everlasting wreath is made of dried blooms, hops *(Humulus)* and love-in-a-mist seedheads *(Nigella damascena)*; and the romantic circlet is decorated with roses *(Rosa)*, masterwort *(Astrantia)* and smoke bush *(Cotinus)* leaves.

EDIBLE VALENTINE

To make the meringue: *beat the egg whites until they are stiff. Add 4 tablespoons/¼ cup of the sugar and whisk again until the mixture is shiny. Fold in the remaining sugar. Draw a heart shape, 10in (25cm) at its widest, on a piece of waxed baking paper. Brush lightly with vegetable oil. Spoon the beaten egg whites into a heart shape about 1in (2.5cm) thick. Spoon meringue around the edge of the heart shape to form deep sides; smooth with a palette knife. Bake in a pre-heated oven 110°C/225°F/Gas Mark ½ for two to three hours until the meringue is crisp. Allow to cool.*

To make the mousse: *cut the passion fruit in half and scoop the orange flesh and black seeds into a basin. Beat the egg yolks and sugar together until they are thick and creamy. Dissolve the gelatine in 4 tablespoons/¼ cup of hot water in a small pan or skillet over a low heat. Do not boil. Stir the passion fruit pulp and gelatine into the egg and sugar mixture. Mix and leave to cool. Whip the cream until it thickens. It should be thick but not stand in peaks. Fold the cream into the passion-fruit mixture. Whip the egg whites until they are stiff and fold them in too. Leave the mousse to set in a soufflé dish or a bowl in the refrigerator.*

Flowers
Lily-of-the-valley *(Convallaria majalis)*
'Baccarolla' rose
(Rosa 'Baccarolla')
'Serena' rose *(Rosa* 'Serena')
Foliage
Galax *(Galax)*
Fruit
Blackberry *(Rubus fruiticosus)*
Red currant *(Ribes rubrum)*
Ingredients
For the meringue:
8 egg whites
500g/1lb caster sugar or
pure cane sugar
vegetable oil
For the mousse:
8 passion fruit
125g/4oz caster sugar or
pure cane sugar
4 eggs, separated
15g/½oz gelatine
300ml/10fl oz/1¼ cups double,
whipping or heavy cream
(The above quantities will serve 6–8)

1 *Assemble the materials (see the previous page). Place the meringue case on a heart-shaped base. To make the base take a piece of thick cardboard and draw around the mould you used to make the meringue. Cut out the heart shape and cover the base with kitchen foil. Place individual galax leaves around the base of the meringue.*

2 *Spoon the passion-fruit mousse into the meringue case until it reaches the rim of the heart. Take sprigs of red currants and lily-of-the-valley, making sure that they are cut to an equal length, and place them with a single pink 'Serena' rose on each alternate galax leaf.*

3 *Now decorate the top. Cover the mousse with the blackberries and 'Serena' roses.*

4 *Cover the rest of the mousse with individual red currants and more 'Serena' roses, making sure that there are no gaps left where the mousse may be visible. The final touch is to add a single deep red 'Baccarolla' rose and a galax leaf. Once you have decorated the meringue with fruit and flowers it will last for one to two hours before the fruits start to stain the white of the meringue heart – it should then be eaten. The finished Edible Valentine arrangement is illustrated opposite.*

The custom of exchanging anonymous love tokens on February 14 is an age-old tradition. In ancient Rome the fertility festival of the Lupercalia fell on February 15 and boys drew girls' names from a love urn. Instead of abandoning this popular pagan custom, the early Christian church instituted it as Saint Valentine's feast day. The flower most instantly associated with this day is, of course, the red rose *(Rosa)*.

Among the many sorts of flowers known to the Romans the rose enjoyed supremacy. Venus, the Roman goddess of love, was said to have used her blood to stain the rose red when she was wounded by one of its thorns, and to this day a blood-red rose is a symbol of love and affection. During the week preceding February 14 you will notice that the price of red roses rises dramatically. Demand for these flowers increases enormously prior to Saint Valentine's Day and because bidding for roses at the international flower auctions is substantially higher in early February than at any other time of the year the final retail prices are forced upward.

During the 19th century strict social conventions restricted communication between lovers and courting couples. For this reason a detailed and symbolic "language of flowers" evolved and various books were published on the subject. Through the giving and receiving of blooms and foliage all sorts of emotions were conveyed and individual plant varieties carried their own particular message. This romantic language of flowers is still recognized by some people today, and comes into play particularly on Saint Valentine's Day and on wedding days, when a bride often chooses a symbolic flower for her bouquet.

For instance, white lilies *(Lilium)* represent purity, bluebells *(Hyacinthoides)* stand for constancy, white camellias *(Camellia)* suggest loveliness, amaryllis *(Hippeastrum)* symbolize pride, daisies *(Bellis)* are for innocence, forget-me-nots *(Myosotis)* indicate true love, ivy *(Hedera)*, which clings to surfaces as it grows, means fidelity, violets *(Viola)* are for modesty, sweet peas *(Lathyrus odoratus)* denote departure, as they are short-lived, and mock orange *(Philadelphus coronarius)*, as its name suggests, means counterfeit.

In general, white blooms symbolize truth, perfection and purity, yellow flowers denote jealousy or falsehood, red petals stand for love and passion and striped flowers such as certain varieties of carnations *(Dianthus)* or tulips *(Tulipa)* suggest refusal. For a Valentine's Day offering you can make tied bunches or posies using symbolic flowers where appropriate. My Edible Valentine heart illustrated on the previous page includes a deep red 'Baccarolla' rose *(Rosa* 'Baccarolla'*)* to symbolize passion, pale pink 'Serena' roses *(Rosa* 'Serena*)* which suggest purity and lily-of-the-valley *(Convallaria majalis)* which signifies the hope of a return to happiness.

In preparation for Saint Valentine's Day I also construct hearts decorated with rose buds and teddy bears shaped from sphagnum moss moulded with small-gauge chicken or mesh wire and bound firmly with reel wire. These gift items require a minimal amount of material but a lot of patience. For the teddy bear you can use a couple of dried cloves for the eyes and perhaps make a pair of small glasses from thick-gauge wire.

For a special Saint Valentine's Day floral gift, instead of offering your loved one the usual bunch of red roses, try making something a little more unusual. To create an everlasting dried Valentine display first take either a piece of flat "designer board" or else a large, flat piece of dry florist's foam (this is either brown or gray in colour); this will be the base of the arrangement. Decide how large you want the finished display to be and cut the base into a square shape accordingly. Then take individual dried pink, red or orange roses (Rosa) and cut the stems short. Insert the roses directly into the base, making a heart shape. Next, surround the central heart with moss, which you can pin into place using U-shaped or German pins. Then add lichen twigs, securing them to the base with florist's wire. I have added rusty metal coils and also four metal hearts to frame the picture. This everlasting Valentine's arrangement can either lie on a flat surface, or else hang from a wall.

M O T H E R ' S   D A Y   N O S E G A Y

1 *Although traditional 19th-century nosegays were wired, this is a simpler unwired version. It is easy to put together and makes an ideal Mother's Day gift. The secret is to choose flowers with different textures and colours so that the rings which make up the nosegay are distinct. The idea of a nosegay is that it is scented, so select fragrant flowers. First condition your cut flowers by snipping their stems and leaving them in nutrient-enriched water for several hours. Strip the leaves off all the stems, but make sure that you remove only the lower leaves from the forget-me-nots and the tulips, otherwise the stems will be very weak. Take a tulip as your middle or focal flower and surround it with a ring of forget-me-nots. Bind the stems together gently with raffia. You can make the nosegay in your hand if this feels comfortable. However, if this feels awkward, take a vase or a glass to hold the flowers as you work.*

2 *Next add a ring of narcissi and then a ring of grape hyacinths to build up the concentric circles which will form the nosegay.*

Flowers
Forget-me-not *(Myotosis)*
Sweet pea *(Lathyrus odoratus)*
Grape hyacinth *(Muscari)*
'Fancy Frill' tulip *(Tulipa 'Fancy Frill')*
'Bridal crown' narcissi
(Narcissus 'Bridal Crown')
Foliage
Galax *(Galax)*

3 *Add a ring of tulips and tie all the stems in the nosegay with a piece of raffia.*

4 *The outer ring of flowers is made of sweet peas. When you have bound the sweet pea stems with raffia, edge the whole bunch with galax leaves. These frame the flowers nicely and also help to protect the flower heads. Bind the stems of the galax leaves with more raffia and make a bow (see Techniques, pages 178-9). Trim all the ends of the*

stems in the nosegay so that it is comfortable to hold in the hand. The finished Mother's Day Nosegay is illustrated opposite.

There are plenty of different flowers you can select to make a scented nosegay or posy. You can use any of the following small, fragrant varieties: polyanthus (Primula polyanthus), primroses (Primula vulgaris), sweet violets (Viola odoratus) – although these will not last long once they have been cut – wax flowers (Stephanotis floribunda), lily-of-the-valley (Convallaria majalis), periwinkles (Vinca major), bluebells (Hyacinthoides campanulatus), cornflowers (Centaurea cyanus), stars of Bethlehem or chincherinchees (Ornithogalum thyrsoides), everlasting peas (Lathyrus latifolius) and freesias (Freesia). You can also select aromatic flowering herbs such as tansy (Tanacetum vulgare), rosemary (Rosmarinus officinalis) and lavender (Lavandula). A single tulip (Tulipa), a rose (Rosa) or perhaps an anemone (Anemone) is suitable as a middle flower.

NEW HOME TOPIARY

Flowers
Dried hydrangea head
(Hydrangea macrophylla)
Glycerined copper beech leaf
(Fagus sylvatica purpurea)
Marjoram or oregano *(Origanum)*
Double-headed sunflower *(Helianthus)*
Sage *(Salvia officinalis)*
Dried poppy seedhead *(Papaver)*
Millet *(Panicum millet)*
Carline thistle *(Carlina)*
Other ingredients
Dried tagliatelle in various colours
Giant cinnamon sticks
(Cinnamomum zeylanicum)
Dried corn on the cob *(Zea mays)*
Dried liquorice sticks *(Glycyrrhiza glabra)*
Dried aniseed *(Pimpinella anisum)*
Pistachio nuts *(Pistacia vera)*

1 *First assemble your materials. You will need a large, sturdy terra-cotta pot as a base, a large dry florist's foam ball (make sure that this is gray or brown and not green – the latter is for arranging fresh flowers), florist's dry-hard clay and some lengths of florist's stub wire for wiring some of the ingredients so that they can be inserted into the foam and held securely.*

2 *Place a lump of dry-hard clay inside the terra-cotta pot, making sure that you fill the pot to approximately 2in (5cm) below the rim so that the base of the topiary tree is stable. Because of the height of the arrangement it will topple over if it is not bottom-heavy. Take some giant cinnamon sticks to form the "trunk" of the topiary tree. Insert the sticks deep into the dry-hard clay while it is still soft and wedge them firmly. The clay will harden quite quickly. Then wedge a large dry foam ball onto the*

exposed ends of the cinnamon sticks. I advise using dry-hard clay as it does not expand and there is little risk of the terra-cotta pot cracking.

3 *Snip the stems off the sunflowers and place them directly into the foam ball, so that the heads are raised approximately 2in (5cm) above the surface of the ball. Group flower heads together so that they have more of an impact when viewed from a distance. Add one large dried hydrangea head and some dried poppy seedheads. If the natural stems do not hold the flower heads in the foam then you should wire the short stems (see Techniques, pages 176-7) in order to strengthen them.*

4 *Group together bunches of sage, dried copper beech leaves and marjoram or oregano by binding the short stems with wire and inserting the wire into the foam. Take some dried maize, wire one end with heavy-gauge wire (see Techniques, page 176)*

and insert. Wire balls of green tagliatelle and insert, (this has to be done with care as the pasta may break). Cut the stems of the thistles short and insert them directly into the foam ball.

5 *Tie some sticks of liquorice into a bundle using a length of string. Carefully wire balls of pink tagliatelle and add them to the foam. Wire and add bunches of millet. Continue to cover the surface of the foam, keeping an even all-round covering of decorative material. Infill any gaps – no part of the foam ball should be visible. If you prefer, you can first cover the entire ball with moss, pinning it with U-shaped (see Techniques, pages 172-3) – this ensures that all the foam is covered. Fill the pot with pistachio nuts and star-shaped dried aniseed so that the dry-hard clay in the pot is concealed. This topiary tree (illustrated opposite) has an edible theme and makes an ideal gift for a kitchen.*

Wreath-making is an age-old craft. In ancient Greece, wreaths of laurel
(Laurus) were awarded to winners of sporting competitions and men were
crowned in laurel for their military exploits. And in Egypt archaeologists
have found remains of rings of flowers buried inside royal pyramids, which
are estimated to be 4,500 years old. The original method of making a
wreath by twining leaves and seedheads into a ring, so preserving them in a
long-lasting arrangement, has changed little over the centuries. During
Roman times wreaths were used to announce the birth of a child – if bound
with ribbon the circle signified a newborn girl and if decorated with olive
leaves it paid tribute to a baby boy. A christening party would be an
appropriate occasion to revive this charming bygone tradition.

For some people the wreath is a funereal kind of flower arrangement.
However, its basic form is so versatile and, depending on the ingredients
used, a ring or circle of plant material can be adapted to suit all sorts of
special occasions and it can be appreciated as a symbol of renewal,
continuity and everlasting life.

Making wreaths or welcome rings offers the flower arranger enormous
scope for creativity and experimentation. The starting point is the base or
frame, which comes in many different forms. It may be a circle of pliable
twigs or vine such as grape *(Vitis vinifera)*, wisteria *(Wisteria)* or honeysuckle
(Lonicera) bound with wire, string or raffia. Or you could use a ready-made
wire base or one made from a coathanger which you can pad with straw or
moss (see page 132) or a ring of florist's wet or dry foam. It is also a nice idea
to bind ribbon around the base to complement the colours of the plant
material to be added. Once you have prepared the base then you can begin
to insert fresh or dried plant material as you require. To do this, follow the
basic wiring techniques illustrated and explained on pages 176-7.

You can hang wreaths on doors, walls or above a mantel shelf, or you
can lay them flat on a surface such as a hall table or in the middle of a festive
kitchen or dining-room table. The advantage of horizontal wreaths is that
you can incorporate candles into the arrangement which, when lit, provide
a special ambience. Remember never to leave lit candles and flammable
plant material unattended. At Yuletide you can make an evergreen base
from fresh-smelling pine *(Pinus)* and wire in all sorts of nuts, rosy apples,
pine cones, berried holly *(Ilex)* and ivy *(Hedera)*. For a Harvest Festival or
Thanksgiving, perhaps make a straw base and decorate it with varnished
gourds *(Cucurbita pepo)* and seasonal fruits or miniature vegetables
reflecting the hues of autumn or fall. To make a culinary wreath for
someone who enjoys cooking, pin moss into a frame with U-shaped pins
and perhaps attach whole cloves of garlic *(Allium sativum)*, colourful
peppers *(Capsicum)*, bay leaves *(Laurus nobilis)* and any kind of aromatic
herbs. Lastly, rings of flowers and leaf can also be worn. For example, you
can embellish the rim of a straw hat with fresh or dried flowers, or construct
a headdress for a bride or a bridesmaid, or make a hoop of flowers for a page
boy to carry in a wedding procession.

*Wreaths or rings of fresh or dried flowers and foliage make suitable gifts for all sorts of
special occasions. I like to construct floral wreaths for happy events such as the birth of a
child. This christening ring would be an ideal offering for a mother and baby and it can
either be laid on a flat surface, perhaps in the middle of a table, or else hung on a wall or a
door. First take a ring of wet florist's foam (these are available from florist's shops and also
from gardening outlets) and soak it in water; this will be the base of the arrangement. Next
attach a piece of wire to the frame so that it forms a loop; this means that the recipient can
hang the wreath if so desired. Add the loop first as it will be difficult to attach once the
wreath is covered. Then begin to arrange your chosen plant material. Here I have used
variegated pittosporum (Pittosporum crassifolium 'Variegatum') to cover the base. Then I
added flowering laurustinus (Viburnum tinus), guelder rose (Viburnum opulus), dill
(Anethum graveolens), white hellebores (Helleborus), ranunculus (Ranunculus) and florets
of delphinium (Delphinium elatum) and hydrangea (Hydrangea macrophylla).*

Techniques

EQUIPMENT

Although it is quite possible to create attractive flower arrangements with a minimum of specialist knowledge, in this chapter all sorts of practical hints and techniques are illustrated and explained that, once mastered, will greatly increase the creative scope of the amateur arranger. The more you develop your skills, the more enjoyment the art of flower arranging will afford. The enormous choice of raw materials available to flower enthusiasts seems to expand continually, with new varieties and equipment appearing on the market every year.

If you live in a rural area and have access to a sizeable garden with enough blooms to bring indoors then you will have a ready source of flowers on your doorstep. And if you live in an urban area then you are likely to have florist shops and flower markets to hand. Whether you grow your own flowers or purchase them from retail or wholesale outlets, many of the items of equipment – or "mechanics" as they are commonly called – which are illustrated on the opposite page will help you to arrange flowers and foliage to professional standards.

One of the most important pieces of equipment is a sharp cutting implement. Scissors or a knife are vital for cutting the ends cleanly off all sorts of stems before arranging them, and secateurs are useful for cutting hard woody stems. If you wish to create a large-scale arrangement using a substantial amount of plant material then I advise standing the stems in water while you work, in order to prevent wilting. It is also useful to prepare the stems on a large piece of plastic sheeting as this protects surfaces and speeds up the clearing away process considerably.

All the items of equipment shown opposite are essential tools of the trade for trained florists and, used correctly, they will enable the amateur to construct either ambitious large-scale displays which won't collapse and will keep their symmetry or else smaller arrangements where every stem will stay in place. Even the most delicate petals and the most unwieldy vegetables can hold their own once you have learnt the basic techniques of wiring.

The mechanics of flower arranging can broadly be divided into two sections – bases and supports.

BASES

Hanging baskets provide a useful base for creating cascading arrangements. Two semi-spherical baskets joined together will make a base for a hanging ball or perhaps a large-scale topiary tree. You can fill the basket with florist's foam or moss and then begin to insert the stems. Half baskets are useful for hanging onto walls. Hanging balls are an attractive option for formal celebrations such as a wedding party.

There are various types of florist's foam. The green foam must be floated on water (do not force it under the water). Once the foam has sunk below the water level and air bubbles cease to rise to the surface then it is ready for arranging (follow the manufacturer's instructions). Green foam can only be soaked once and because it absorbs water it keeps fresh stems moist. Make sure that the foam remains moist by

topping it up with water when necessary. However, most stems will last less long in wet foam than in water. Brown or gray foam is for dried flower arranging and dry-foam balls are ideal for making pomanders. Both types of foam come in various shapes and sizes, including bricks, rings, balls, cones, flat "designer" boards which can be cut into any shape and also crosses for making sympathy flowers. Some also have suction pads and can be hung on a wall.

While a foam base is designed to support even the most delicate stems, heavy-stemmed flowers and foliage are best arranged in a base made of medium-gauge chicken or mesh wire crumpled into a loose ball and placed inside a container. However, chicken wire looks unsightly in a glass or transparent container. Medium-gauge chicken wire is suitable for most types of stems; if the gauge is too small then it will be difficult to insert the stems. Plastic-coated chicken wire protects the stems from tearing.

Other useful bases include plastic trays, bowls and pew ends or small-spray trays with handles for church decoration – these come in various shapes and sizes and are often moulded to neatly accommodate florist's foam. The florist's spike or "frog" can be stuck onto the bottom of a plastic tray or bowl – a piece of florist's foam is then wedged onto the spike and the "frog" holds the foam firmly in place. If the spike does not have a self-adhesive base then a small ball of florist's fix – a waterproof clay-like substance, will hold the spike in place.

Pin holders are usually made of heavy metal and placed in the bottom of a vase, they provide a stable base for inserting stems. The spikes in the pin holder or the deeper-sided well pin hold the stems in place and they are particularly useful for creating ikebana or Japanese-style arrangements. However, flower stems do not benefit from this kind of support.

If you wish to decorate a candlestick or a candelabra with flowers for a special occasion, start by inserting a candle cup into the hole where the candle is normally placed. Then attach a block of green florist's foam into the moulded candle cup using florist's tape – the foam provides a large base to cover with flowers and foliage. Insert a florist's candle holder into the foam: this will hold the candle.

SUPPORTS

Stub wires come in various thicknesses or gauges, starting with very fine rose wire which is suitable for wiring the most delicate flowers and leaves as well as individual florets of larger flowers for bridal work, for instance in corsages and headdresses. Small blooms wired into a bouquet or a headdress must not be over-wired otherwise they will look stiff and unnatural. Medium-gauge wires are suitable for supporting all kinds of medium-sized flowers and heavy-gauge wire is necessary for large flower heads and fruits and vegetables which can be weighty.

Previous page: To make a hanging ball bind moss with reel wire and frame the whole with chicken wire. Then wire and insert a variety of large-headed flowers.

While stub wires act as reinforced stems, reel wire is useful for all kinds of binding work. Very fine reel wire or silver wire is suitable for binding very light plant material and is used primarily in bridal work, such as adding wired flowers into a bouquet or a headdress. Thick reel wire will secure all sorts of heavy items. Medium-gauge reel wire is useful for binding moss onto a wreath base or for constructing the base of a hanging ball or for adding to a garland. You can make almost any shape by sculpting moss with reel wire, including hearts for Valentine's day and teddy bears or other animals for children. Reel wire is also frequently used for grouping bunches of foliage or flowers into sprigs before adding them to an arrangement. Grouping plant material gives it more visual impact in an arrangement.

To supplement the support of wiring you can use pins. For example, if you wish to pin a large clump of moss to a base, take a heavy stub wire and bend it into a hairpin or U-shape (see page 177). Smaller U-shaped German pins will hold leaves onto a base such as a wreath or a ball. And pretty pearl-headed pins are useful for pinning a buttonhole or a corsage to a lapel or perhaps attaching a garland of light trails of ivy to a table cloth for a wedding party.

In addition to binding stems with wire, string, rope, raffia or ribbon all fulfil the same purpose. There are various types of florist's tape available. These specialist tapes are waterproof and so adhere even if they come into contact with water or moisture. Florist's tapes come in various widths and colours; I tend to use dark green tape which is least conspicuous and resembles the natural colour of stems. I use wide tape for securing blocks of florist's foam to, for instance, a large pedestal and thinner tape for attaching foam to a candle cup. Narrow green tape is useful for concealing wired stems and sharp exposed wire ends, especially in bridal work. Brown tape is suitable for concealing wiring on dried flower stems. I also find double-sided tape very useful. Because it is adhesive on both sides I often cover a container with double-sided tape and then decorate it with leaves, twigs, bamboo, small vegetables and seedheads. Florist's tie tape is transparent and useful for binding a gift bouquet wrapped in cellophane.

Garden canes come in various lengths and thicknesses and provide useful support for long, weak stems which tend to flop or break. For a large-scale arrangement it is possible to lengthen stems to suit the proportion of the display by attaching a cone or funnel to a piece of garden cane or bamboo with tape; then simply insert the stem into the cone.

Lastly, if you wish to make a topiary tree then dry-hard clay – which acts like quick-drying cement – will support the weight of the tree "trunk" and the topiary itself. When not in use, the clay will stay soft and malleable if completely wrapped in plastic; when exposed to the air it turns hard. Wedge enough clay to fill a sturdy container and insert the "trunk" into the clay. Dry-hard clay is easy and clean to use, it also has the advantage that, unlike cement and plaster of Paris it does not expand when it dries, so there is little risk of it cracking the container.

Half hanging basket

Wet foam brick

Chicken wire

Garden canes

Stub wire

Rose wire

Florist's wire

Well pin holder

Foam ring

Florist's tapes

Knife

Pew end
or small spray tray

Pin holder

Spike or "frog"

Scissors

String

German pins

Florist's fix

Bowl base

Pearl-headed pins

Secateurs

Silver wire

Dry-hard clay

Candle cup

Reel or blue wire

Tie tape

Candle holder

Rope

Ribbon

Double-sided tape

Dry foam ball

Cone or funnel

If roses wilt prematurely, try recutting the stems. As a last resort, wrap the heads in paper to protect against steam and plunge the stem ends into boiling water for 10 seconds.

Sadly, violets (Viola) wilt all too quickly. To revive them for making a posy or a small bunch immerse the flowers completely in water for up to one hour.

Tulip (Tulipa) stems tend to bend. To prevent this wrap the flowers in paper (which absorbs water) and place in a bucket of water overnight in a cool room.

TREATMENT OF STEMS

Before you begin to arrange cut flowers and foliage in a clean, germ-free container it is important to prepare the stems in the correct way so that the arrangement lasts as long as possible. The first step is to allow the stems to drink in deep water (preferably nutrient-enriched with a commercial cut-flower feed) for several hours. This initial drink revives the plant material and also allows the stems to firm up – which is particularly important if you are arranging in a wet-foam base where stems cannot drink freely.

Always snip the ends off stems before arranging them, as this helps them to take up water with maximum efficiency. Different types of stems require different treatments in order to prolong life (see the illustration below). A stem end which has lost its green colour – this is common with, for example

daffodils (*Narcissus*) – must be removed, as the white part will not draw water. Also, you should leave sappy stems such as euphorbias (*Euphorbia*) to soak before arranging them, otherwise the oozing liquid will contaminate the water in the container – in glass receptacles this looks unsightly. Where stems have hard nodules, for example carnations (*Dianthus*), make a snip above, and not immediately below, a nodule in order to facilitate drinking.

Below (left to right): Various stem treatments have been used in the past, from cutting at an angle, flattening with a hammer and splitting with a knife. Latest research suggests that all stems respond best to a simple diagonal cut. For hollow stems (second from right), fill with water and plug with cotton wool. Poppies (far right) benefit from singeing with a flame or dipping in boiling water for 5 seconds.

If you find cut flowers are wilting, perhaps after transportation, then you can revive them by various methods (see the illustrations above). Running cool water over the stems and spraying the petals with a mister spray will also help to prevent wilting. Also, you can greatly improve the appearance of tired gray (not green) foliage by submerging the leaves completely under water. It is possible to clean dusty gray leaves with warm water mixed with liquid detergent and polish shiny leaves with a dab of cooking oil.

The tightly closed uppermost buds of a stem rarely open before the lower buds have bloomed and died. For this reason you should snip off the topmost buds which will take away water from the rest of the stem. I also advise removing the stamens from lilies (*Lilium*) as these tend to stain the petals and anything else they come into contact with!

1 *Anemones (Anemone), or windflowers as they are also sometimes called, have beautiful cupped heads which tend to flatten as they mature. To make a hand-tied bunch choose long stems – these are easier to work with – and make sure that the petals are not more than half open, otherwise the bunch will not last well. Begin by grouping the stems in one hand, adding further stems at an angle.*

2 *This kind of bunch is most effective when made with a mixture of different coloured blooms such as pinks, reds, blues, mauves and purples. With one hand continue to add long stems diagonally to the bunch which is held securely in the other hand. It is important not to hold the bunch too tightly in order to retain the spiral shape. Position the heads of the flowers into an even dome.*

3 *Continue adding more long stems to the spiral until it is no longer possible to hold all the stems in one hand. At this point tie the bunch tightly with a length of raffia or string at the narrowest part of the spiral, just below the dome of flower heads. Then cut all the stems ends to an even length. If the bunch is correctly made then it will stand upright without support, like a sheaf of corn.*

1 *To make a bunch using large flowers with long stems it is easier to cross the stems than it is to spiral them neatly as illustrated above. Instead of spiralling the stems, concentrate on positioning the flower heads and foliage, which should be built up from the middle outward in an even all-round bunch. Start by selecting the longest stems and group them closely together to form the core of the bunch.*

2 *Add individual stems of lilies (Lilium), euphorbia (Euphorbia), dill (Anethum graveolens), pussy willow (Salix), eucalyptus (Eucalyptus) and bear grass (Dasylirion) with one hand, to the bunch which should be held tightly in the other hand. You can either add stems to the outside of the bunch or else insert them from above. Build up an even all-round bunch as you work.*

3 *When the bunch becomes too heavy to hold in one hand, tie all the stems together tightly with a length of string or raffia at the narrowest part of the bunch – just below the dome of flower heads. Make sure that the bunch is evenly balanced when viewed from all sides. The bunch does not need to be too neat; so allow the wispy bear grass to fall naturally and so break any rigidity of outline.*

1. Wiring a delicate slipper orchid (Cypripedium).

2. A single leg-mounted safflower (Carthamus).

3. External wiring on a freesia (Freesia).

WIRING TECHNIQUES

1 To wire an orchid insert a fine wire into the stem. Hook the wire and pull down into the petals. Secure the hooked wire to the stem with a second wire.

2 To single leg-mount a small flower take a medium-gauge wire and bend the top 1in (2.5cm) into a U-shape. Bind the U-end and the cut-off stem together with the long end of the same wire.

3 Wind fine silver wire through a delicate flower head until it provides the support you require. Then take a medium-gauge wire and make a double leg-mount (see 13) to act as a reinforced stem.

4 To wire a pine cone wrap heavy-gauge wire around the base and twist the wire tightly so that it cannot slip off the cone. To wire walnuts *(Juglans regia)* either find a weak point in the joint of the nut and insert heavy-gauge wire or coil one end of a stub wire and glue it to the base of the nut.

5 Wire a pomegranate *(Punica granatum)* by inserting heavy-gauge wire through the skin and

flesh of the base, then twist the two ends together. Smaller vegetables such as peppers *(Capsicum)* can be double leg-mounted with a medium-gauge wire (see 13). To wire a miniature aubergine *(Solanum)* pierce the base with a single leg-mount using a medium-gauge wire (see 2). To wire a miniature pineapple *(Ananas)* insert a heavy-gauge wire straight into the base.

6 To neaten a rosebud make small U-shaped pins from fine wire and pin the sepals into the petals.

7 Thread a fine wire through the base of a floret and bind it to the cut-off stem with a double leg mount, using silver or rose wire (see 13).

8 To attach a large clump of fresh moss to a base bend heavy-gauge wire into a hairpin.

9 Insert a medium-gauge wire straight up the stem of a carnation *(Dianthus)* and hook the end. Pull the hook down so that it is embedded in the petals. Take a second, thinner wire and bind the calyx of the flower and the medium-gauge wire together.

10 Flowers such as gerberas *(Gerbera)* with smooth, straight stems lend themselves to external wiring. Insert one end of a medium-gauge wire into the calyx and spiral the wire down the stem.

11 This wired anemone *(Anemone)* is neatened with green tape which simulates the natural stem.

12 This pygmy amaryllis *(Hippeastrum)* is well supported with a strong wire inserted into its hollow stem. Use a garden cane to support a large amaryllis.

13 The double leg-mount technique is useful for supporting all sorts of heavy flower heads. Double a length of heavy-gauge wire and place the U-end of the wire against the cut-off stem. Wind one half of the double leg around the other. This method extends the stem by two "legs" of wire.

14 To wire foliage such as ivy *(Hedera)* for bridal work "stitch" fine silver or rose wire through the central vein which is situated at the back of the leaf. Join the two wire ends together and twist them around the cut-off leaf stem.

4. Methods of wiring pine cones and nuts with heavy-gauge stub wire.

5. Wired fruits and vegetables, including miniature varieties.

6. *How to neaten a rosebud (Rosa) with pins.*

7. *Wiring a hyacinth (Hyacinthus) floret.*

8. *A heavy hairpin wire holds moss in place.*

9. *A hook-wired carnation (Dianthus).*

10. *External wiring on a gerbera (Gerbera).*

11. *A wired stem concealed with green tape.*

12. *Strong wire inserted into a hollow stem.*

13. *A double leg-mounted thistle (Echinops).*

14. *A stitched single ivy (Hedera) leaf.*

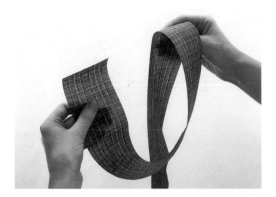  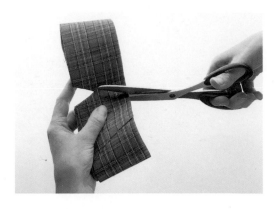

1 *First select a length of ribbon, made of paper or of fabric. Here I have used a tartan patterned fabric. Make sure that the length of ribbon is not too short. Decide how large you wish the loops of the finished bow to be. Hold one end of the ribbon in one hand and make a loop with the other hand.*

2 *Fold the ribbon over itself four times into one loop. The size of this loop will determine the finished size of the bow. Take a pair of sharp scissors and snip the end of the ribbon. Looping the ribbon four times over itself will produce a bow of eight loops. Six folds will produce twelve loops etc.*

3 *Once the ribbon is neatly folded, hold it tightly in one hand and using a pair of sharp scissors make a V-shaped snip in the middle of the folded ribbon – this will form the middle of the bow. Do not allow the two V-shaped snips to meet in the middle; avoid cutting them too close.*

PRESENTATION

When you arrange flowers and foliage to give to someone then a little extra time spent on presentation will greatly enhance the finished effect of your floral gift. Careful wrapping also protects flowers during transportation and ensures that they reach their destination in good condition.

Most gift flowers require transporting of some kind. If the journey between giver and recipient is a long one then the cut stems should be kept in a container half-filled with water. Make sure that the receptacle is firmly wedged and cannot topple over. If you are transporting delicate flowers then you can mould a piece of large-gauge chicken or mesh wire over the mouth of a container – this will support the flower heads while allowing the stems to drink.

Alternatively you can transport blooms laid flat in a box. Do not overfill the box with cut stems otherwise they may become damaged and will tend to smother each other. Wrap delicate blooms in damp tissue paper (using a mister spray) to keep them moist. In order to dress up a box cover it with brown paper or gift wrap. Choose gift wrap which complements the hues of the flowers.

Right: To transport cut flowers I wrap the stems in tissue paper dampened with a mister spray and place them carefully into a box lined with tissue paper and covered in brown wrapping. Do not spray orchids as the petals turn transparent.

1 *To make a three-loop bow start by selecting a length of ribbon, made of paper or fabric. Make sure the ribbon is long enough. I prefer to use a wide fabric ribbon. Start at one end of the length of ribbon and pinch it in two places using the thumb and forefinger of each hand – the distance between each hand determines the size of the loop.*

2 *Transfer the pinched point of the ribbon in your right hand to the pinched point of the ribbon held in your left hand. Hold both pinched points tightly together in your left hand – this forms the middle of the bow. With your right hand pinch the ribbon again to begin to make the second loop of the bow. Keep each loop the same size.*

3 *Continue to make loops of the same size with your right hand by pinching the ribbon and transferring each individual pinched point of the ribbon to the left hand so that the ribbon naturally forms a loop. Hold the pinched parts tightly in the left hand. Make a total of six loops in this way so that both halves of the bow comprise three loops.*

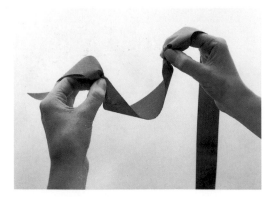  

4 *Cut a length of the same ribbon to half its width and place it in-between the two V-shaped snips. Then tie the strip of ribbon into a tight double knot so that the finished bow is secure and will not come loose. Pull the two ends of the narrower ribbon in opposite directions with both hands.*

5 *Now start to give the bow shape. With one hand hold the middle of the bow – where the narrower strip of ribbon forms a central knot. With the other hand start to separate each of the four layers of folded ribbon in the original loop. Separate the four loops on one side of the central knot first.*

6 *Continue to separate the rest of the loops with one hand while holding the middle of the bow with the other hand. Separate all eight loops and shape them so that the outline of the finished bow resembles a pompom. Attach the bow to a bouquet or a bunch with the two narrower strips of ribbon.*

Left: This hand-held bunch of pink and blue flowers is wrapped in cellophane so that the beauty of the blooms is fully visible. The flower heads are uncovered to allow them to breathe and their scent to escape. I have used a wire-edged ribbon which shapes into a bow.

Long-stemmed bunches of flowers transport well protected in a loose spiral of tissue paper covered with gift wrap – this also serves to hide the stems. Short-stemmed bunches and posies look attractive wrapped in cellophane as the blooms remain visible. With a small or medium-sized bunch leave the flower heads exposed. However, it is best to cover a large presentation bouquet entirely with cellophane to protect the blooms and you should make small breathing holes in the wrapping to prevent the flowers from becoming too hot which causes wilting as well as condensation. It is best to wrap flowers just before transportation or presentation as they do not benefit from being out of water. Full-blown flowers will not travel well so use blooms which are in bud or half-open. Also, remove the stamens from flowers such as lilies *(Lilium)* as these stain.

Once you have wrapped your posy, bunch or bouquet the finishing touch is to add a bow. There are many different techniques for making bows using ribbons of different widths and types of fabric or you can use sea grass rope, string or raffia. I also like to plait fronds of grasses such as bear grass *(Dasylirion)* to use instead of a bow.

4 *When you have finished making six loops of a similar size and all the pinched points of the ribbon are held tightly in your left hand, take a pair of sharp scissors and snip the end of the ribbon after the last loop at an angle. Adjust each of the loops with your right hand so that the bow is symmetrical and rounded in shape.*

5 *Still holding the bow tightly with the thumb and forefinger of your left hand, take a piece of the same ribbon with your right hand and place it over the middle of the bow at the point where all the loops meet. You will now need to call upon an extra pair of hands to accomplish the final part of making the bow.*

6 *While you hold all the loops tightly together in your left hand ask someone to tie the short piece of ribbon tightly around the middle of the bow where all the loops meet. Adjust the loops again so that the bow is rounded and symmetrical. Use the piece of ribbon securing the middle of the bow to tie around a bunch or a bouquet.*

Gazetteer

A

Acacia
Mimosa
Ball-shaped clusters of very fragrant tiny sulphur-yellow flowers. Tender shrub with sensitive leaves.
CARE Plunge the stem ends in warm water with flower food.

Acanthus
Acanthus
Tall stems of mauve and white prickly flower bracts. Useful in dried-flower arrangements.
CARE Slit the stem ends and plunge in tepid water.

Acer
Maple
Very varied foliage plants, from deeply cut purple leaves to palmate green leaves that are edged with yellow.
CARE Slit woody stem ends and place in deep water.

Achillea
Achillea
Tall, feathery-leaved plants topped with saucer-like heads of yellow flowers. Flower heads are attractive dried for decoration in winter. Fern-like foilage.
CARE Cut stem ends.

Acidanthera
Acidanthera
Fragrant, lily-like white flowers with strongly contrasting basal blotches.
CARE Place in deep water for a few hours before arranging.

Aconitum
Monkshood
Plants with spikes of blue helmet-shaped flowers along with finely-segmented leaves that are mostly rounded.
CARE Cut stem ends.

Adiantum
Maidenhair Fern
Foliage plants with slender delicate-looking stems of fan-shaped, light-green fronds.
CARE Seal stem ends with a naked flame.

Aesculus
Horse Chestnut
Broad palmate leaves, with tall candles of cream, white, crimson, pink or yellow flowers, followed in autumn by large, round mahogany-coloured "conkers".
CARE Slit stem ends and place in deep water.

Agapanthus
African Lily
Although white flowers are available, blue-violet varieties are especially attractive. Broad, dark-green leaves.
CARE Place in deep water for a few hours before arranging.

Ageratum
Ageratum
Short to medium-tall plants with quilled florets of blue, purple, pink or white flowers. These are not long-lasting once they have been cut.
CARE Remove lower leaves.

Alchemilla
Lady's Mantle
Very popular, yellowy green feathery flowers which have softly rounded green leaves.
CARE Cut stem ends and place in deep water before arranging.

Allium
Onion head
Long-lasting, ball-shaped heads of flowers in green, white, purple, blue or pink. with narrow, basal leaves.
CARE Place in deep water and change water regularly.

Aloe
Aloe
Tall, thick fleshy leaves that form large rosettes which have spikes of either red or yellow flowers.
CARE Cut stems at an angle.

Alpinia
Ginger Lily
Leafy-stemmed herb which is often grown for its large ornamental foliage.
CARE Cut stems at an angle.

Alstroemeria
Alstroemeria
Orange, yellow, pink, white or red trumpet-shaped flowers. Attractive seed pods are an additional bonus.
CARE Place stems in deep water with cut-flower feed.

Althaea
Hollyhock
Long stems of single or double flowers in crimson, pink, white or yellow.
CARE Plunge stem ends in boiling water for 10 seconds.

Amaranthus
Love-lies-bleeding
Long-lasting tassels of crimson-coloured flowers. Oval, pale-green leaves.
CARE Remove lower leaves, cut the stem ends and plunge in deep water.

Amaryllis
Belladonna Lily
Clusters of trumpet-shaped flowers, either pink or white on a purple stem.
CARE Place in deep water for a few hours before arranging.

Ananas
Pineapple
Rosette of spiny leaves which surrounds a tall stalk and is topped with a large tropical fruit.
CARE Cut stems straight across.

Anemone coronaria
Anemone
Shallow cup-shaped flowers in shades of red, pink, blue or purple which often have contrasting centres. Parsley-like leaves.
CARE Cut stem ends.

Anemone japonica
Japanese Anemone
Long straight stems of shaped flowers. These are available in shades of pink, lilac or white.
CARE Cut the stem ends at an angle.

Anethum
Dill
Aromatic foliage plant with finely cut thread-like leaves.
CARE Cut the stem ends and place these in water.

Angelica
Angelica
Statuesque herb-garden plant with bright-green foliage and white or green flowers.
CARE Plunge stem ends in boiling water for 10 seconds.

Anigozanthos
Kangaroo Paw
Long-lasting cream or yellow flower trumpets useful in dried-flower arrangements.
CARE Cut stems once a week to aid water uptake.

Anthemis
Camomile
Foliage plant with finely cut strongly scented leaves. White, daisy-like flowers that have yellow centres.
CARE Remove lower leaves and place in cool position.

Anthriscus
Cow Parsley
Long-lasting umbels of small white flowers and deeply cut fern-like leaves.
CARE Plunge the stem ends in boiling water.

Anthurium
Painter's Palette
Exotic-looking scarlet spathe with a prominent yellow spadix. The plant has large dark-green leaves.
CARE Place in deep water for a few hours before arranging.

Antirrhinum
Snapdragon
Clusters of brightly coloured flowers, each being hinged to give a mouth-like effect.
CARE Cut stem ends and place in deep water.

Aquilegia
Colombine
Bonnet-shaped flowers with long spurs are available in a wide range of mixed colours.
CARE Put in deep water for a few hours before arranging. Do not leave out of water for long.

Artemisia
Artemisia
Attractive plant with deeply cut silver-gray foliage. Some with small cream flowers.
CARE Cut stem ends and plunge in deep water.

Arundinaria
Bamboo
Tall-stemmed foliage plant with slender grassy leaves.
CARE Keep plant away from sunlight.

Asclepias
Silk Weed
Clusters of small, trumpet-like orange, purple or white flowers on tall stems. This is not long-lasting once cut.
CARE Remove lower foliage and cut stems at an angle. Prone to wilt if left in sun.

Asparagus
Asparagus Fern
Foliage plant that has delicate feathery leaves.
CARE Plunge the stem ends in deep water.

Aster
Michaelmas Daisy
Long-lasting flowers in blue, white, pink or violet, with either yellow or orange centres.
CARE Cut stem ends and place in deep water. Remove the lower foliage.

Astilbe
Astilbe
Arching, feathery, tapering plumes in red, crimson, pink, white or lilac in summer. Brown flowers in winter.
CARE Cut stems and place in deep water for a few hours if stems are limp. Do not leave the plant in direct sunlight.

Astrantia
Astrantia
Long-lasting pinkish-tinged, greenish-white bracts with mid-green leaves variegated with cream and yellow.
CARE Place in cool water.

Aucuba
Aucuba
Oval, glossy-green leaves, some with yellow variegation. Also has small, star-shaped purple flowers.
CARE Cut and slit stem ends.

Avena
Common Oat
Grass-like plant with attractive seed heads.
CARE Place in deep water for a few hours before arranging.

B

Ballota
Ballota
Woolly textured foliage plant with round gray-green leaves.
CARE Plunge the stem ends in deep water.

Banksia
Banksia
Dense spikes of spirally placed blooms coloured in either red or yellow. Leaves are long and serrated.
CARE Cut woody stem ends.

Begonia
Begonia
Bright pink, orange, yellow, red or white single or double blooms on fleshy stems. Or, foliage plants with large, heart-shaped green leaves marked in bronze or purple.
CARE Cut stem ends and place in deep water.

Berberis
Berberis
Profuse black or red fruits and small flowers, usually yellow-orange in colour. The evergreen leaves of this plant are small and glossy.
CARE Cut woody stem ends and place in deep water.

Bergenia
Bergenia
Drooping racemes of purple or pink flowers and wide oval-shaped leaves; green in spring and tinged with crimson or coral in autumn or fall. Leathery, toothed leaves.
CARE Submerge leaves in water for a few hours before arranging.

Betula
Birch
Excellent autumn foliage colour and also attractive architectural stems.
CARE Slit stem ends and place in deep water for a few hours.

Borago
Borage
Saucer-shaped flowers opening pink before they eventually turn blue.
CARE Cut stems straight across.

Bouvardia
Bouvardia
Small star-shaped flowers in red, yellow or white.
CARE Cut stem ends and place in deep water. Use cut-flower feed. Never allow the stem ends to dry out and remove the lower foliage to improve longevity.

Brassica
Ornamental Cabbage
These attractive cabbages are in a variety of shades from white to red, with curly edged and deeply cut leaf margins.
CARE Soak entire leaf in cool water before arranging.

Briza
Quaking Grass
Long-lasting, cocoon-shaped seed heads on slender grassy stems. Can be used dried.
CARE Place in deep water.

Brodiaea
Brodiaea
Erect, funnel-shaped flowers, often blue-violet, poised on long and delicate stems. Narrow basal leaves.
CARE Place in water overnight.

Buddleia
Buddleia
Clusters of small, often fragrant, spikes or globes of gold-throated flowers in white, mauve, purple or orange. Large leaves.
CARE Plunge stem ends in boiling water for 10 seconds and then in deep water overnight.

Bupleurum
Bupleurum
Heads of creamy-yellow flowers with glossy blue-green leaves.
CARE Cut stem ends and place in deep water before arranging. Do not allow stems to dry out and remove lower foliage.

Buxus
Box
Foliage plant with tightly packed shiny-green leaves. Flowers are insignificant.
CARE Slit stem ends and place in water.

C

Caladium
Caladium
Large, heart-shaped green leaves, with veining of white, pink or orange.
CARE Plunge stem ends in boiling water for 10 seconds, then submerge leaves in cool water.

Calendula
Marigold
Ball- or daisy-like flowers in shades of gold, yellow, apricot, cream and even white. Lance-shaped, pale-green leaves.
CARE Remove lower leaves and cut with a slant.

Callicarpa
Callicarpa
Small pink or lilac flowers and purple or lilac fruits. Autumn leaf colour is also useful.
CARE Cut woody stem ends and place in deep water.

Callistemon
Bottle-brush
Large, showy brush-like clusters of small red or yellow flowers.
CARE Cut woody stem ends and place in deep water for a few hours before arranging.

Callistephus
China Aster
Daisy-like single or double flowers in purple, blue, red, pink, cream or white.
CARE Cut stem ends and place in deep water before arranging.

Camellia
Camellia
Glossy-green oval-shaped leaves with rounded single or double flowers in an array of colours.
CARE Cut stem ends and place in deep water before arranging.

Campanula
Bellflower
Profuse clusters of bell-shaped flowers in shades of mauve, blue or white. Flowers of different species vary greatly in shape, size and colour.
CARE Place in deep water for a few hours before arranging.

Capsicum
Ornamental Chilli Pepper
Small red or green shiny fruits on the stem.
CARE Cut with a slant and plunge into cool water.

Carthamus
Safflower
Disc-shaped. bright-orange flowers and ovate leaves.
CARE Place in deep water for a few hours. Remove the lower foliage.

Ceanothus
Californian Lilac
Not a true lilac. Dense showy clusters of flowers in various shades of blue, violet, mauve, pink and purple on strong stems. White and grayish tones appear also.
CARE Slit stem ends.

Celosia
Cock's Comb
Brilliant crests or plumes that have deep red, orange, crimson or yellow flowers.
CARE Cut stem ends and place in water. Remove all foliage.

Centaurea
Cornflower
Round, brightly coloured flowers with ruffled petals, in either blue, pink, mauve or white.
CARE Remove lower leaves and cut stem ends. Change water frequently.

Centranthus
Valerian
Dense heads of small white, red or pink fragrant flowers.
CARE Plunge stem ends in boiling water for about 10 seconds and then leave to drink overnight in tepid water.

Chaenomeles
Flowering Quince
Leafless stems of salmon or orange-red flowers which have bright yellow stamens.
CARE Cut stem ends.

Chamaelaucium
Chamaelaucium
Heather-like foliage and white, red or pink flowers.
CARE Cut stem ends.

Cheiranthus
Wallflower
Spikes of fragrant, brightly coloured flowers in bronze, purple, orange, red or yellow.
CARE Remove lower leaves and cut stem ends.

Chionodoxa
Glory-of-the-snow
White, blue or pale-pink star-like flowers on short stems with sparse foilage.
CARE Place in deep water.

Choisya
Mexican Orange Blossom
Clusters of white, sweetly scented, star-shaped flowers framed by shiny green leaves.
CARE Cut woody stem ends.

Chrysanthemum
Chrysanthemum
Long-lasting blooms. Many different colours in a wide range of shapes and sizes.
CARE Cut stem ends, remove lower leaves and change water regularly. Use flower food for maximum life.

Cirsium
Plumed Thistle
Stems of multi-headed, thistle-like flowers in purple, crimson or white. Buy only when buds are opening.
CARE Cut stem ends and place in water with cut-flower feed. Remove foliage.

Clematis
Clematis
Very varied flower shape, size and colour. Most have bell-shaped flowers with four pointed petals.
CARE Seal stem ends with a naked flame.

Clivia
Kaffir Lily
Fleshy spikes topped with clusters of bell-shaped orange flowers with yellow throats. Long-lasting as cut flowers.
CARE Cut stem ends; put in deep water for a few hours before arranging.

Cobaea
Cobaea
Stems of large violet or green bell-shaped flowers with prominent calyx.
CARE Cut stem ends diagonally and put in water.

Convallaria
Lily-of-the-valley
Fragrant, bell-shaped white flowers on graceful stems.
CARE Cut stem ends and place in deep water before arranging. Do not allow stem ends to dry.

Comus
Dogwood
Stems in red, purple or yellow. Some with large bracts in white, pink or yellow. Foliage also attractive.
CARE Slit woody stem ends and plunge in water.

Corylopsis
Winter Hazel
Racemes of small, yellow fragrant flowers appear on bare stems, followed by strongly veined leaves.
CARE Slit stem ends and place in deep water.

Cosmos
Cosmos
Graceful disc-shaped, brightly coloured flowers and fern-like foliage. Range of warm tones, either single shade or striped.
CARE Place in deep water for a few hours before arranging.

Cotinus
Smoke Bush
Valuable foliage plant with purple, disc-shaped leaves.
CARE Cut woody stem ends and plunge in water. Remove soft and lower foliage.

Craspedia
Craspedia
Dense globular heads of yellow flowers carried on long leafless stems. Good in dried-flower arrangements.
CARE Cut stems straight across.

Crocosmia
Montbretia
Arching sprays of orange or yellow flowers.
CARE Place in deep water for a few hours before arranging. Very sensitive to ethylene gas (as emitted by bananas) and should be kept away from fruit, vegetables and dying flowers.

Crocus
Crocus
Delicate, brightly coloured flowers, similar in shape to a narrow wine flute. Silver-striped leaves. Colours include mauve, blue, white, cream, yellow and beige – as well as multi-coloured stipes.
CARE Place in deep water.

Cryptomeria
Japanese Cedar
Coniferous plants with fresh-green foliage in spring, followed by bronze-coloured foliage in autumn or fall.
CARE Cut woody stem ends and place in deep water.

Cucurbita
Gourd
Large ornamental fruits, basically oval in shape, and usually yellow, green or orange, sometimes also with stripes.
CARE Preserve by varnishing.

Cyclamen
Cyclamen
Single stems of pink, purple, rose or white flowers with strongly reflexed petals.
CARE Cut stem ends and place in deep water before arranging.

Cymbidium
Cymbidium
This popular orchid has long-lasting blooms opening in succession along erect or drooping stems. Colours include white, yellow, green, pink, red and mahogany.
CARE Cut stem ends at angle; cut again every few days.

Cynara
Globe Artichoke
Large globe-like flowers in green or blue. Useful in dried-flower arrangements.
CARE Plunge stem ends in boiling water.

Cyperus
Papyrus Grass
Umbels of long, grass-like leaves on tall, erect stems.
CARE Place in deep water.

Cypripedium
Slipper Orchid
Graceful stems of single flowers, varying greatly in size, shape and colour.
CARE Cut stem ends at angle and cut again every few days.

Cytisus
Broom
Stems of pea-shaped flowers commonly yellow but also cream, pink or crimson.
CARE Cut stem ends and plunge in boiling water for a few seconds.

D

Dahlia
Dahlia
Popular, long-stemmed flowers in a wide range of colours, shapes and sizes. Leaves are generally oval and in mid-green.
CARE Remove leaves and plunge stem ends in deep water.

Dasylirion
Bear Grass
A tree-like plant related to the yucca. Leaves are long and glossy green with spiny margins.
CARE Clean soil from stems and cut off white ends.

Daucus
Queen Anne's Lace
Umbels of small white flowers arranged in lace-like patterns, with feathery foliage.
CARE Cut stem ends and place in deep water.

Delphinium
Delphinium
Impressively tall stems with spikes of cup-shaped, sometimes hooded and spurred, flowers that are usually blue or white.
CARE Cut stem ends and change water daily.

Dendrobium
Singapore Orchid
Stems of flowers often with strongly coloured fringed lips.
CARE Cut stem ends at an angle; cut again every few days.

Dianthus
Carnation
Long-lasting, often fragrant, flowers that are commonly red, pink or white.
CARE Cut stems at an angle between nodes. Place in water with cut-flower feed overnight.

Dicenta
Bleeding Heart
Pink and white heart-shaped flowers on arching stems. Fern-like, mid-green foilage.
CARE Place in warm water.

Digitalis
Foxglove
Tall spikes of thimble-shaped flowers, often spotted inside. Oval, deep-green leaves.
CARE Place in warm water for a few hours before arranging.

Dipsacus
Teasel
Tall prickly stems topped with shiny bracts that contain small lilac-coloured flowers.
CARE Plunge stem ends in boiling water; change water regularly.

Doronicum
Leopard's Bane
Yellow, daisy-like flowers on long stems. Heart-shaped, bright-green leaves.
CARE Place in warm water for a few hours before arranging.

E

Echinops
Globe Thistle
Silver-blue, spiky flower heads on rigid sturdy stems.
CARE Cut at an angle and place in deep water. Remove lower foliage.

Elaeagnus
Elaeagnus
Foliage plants with shiny, often variegated leaves.
CARE Slit stem ends and change water frequently.

Episcia dianthiflora
Lace Flower
Sprays of small white flowers with prominent stamens. Thick velvety leaves.
CARE Cut stems straight across.

Eremurus
Foxtail Lily
Closely packed spikes of flowers in yellow, white or shades of orange.
CARE Place in deep water for a few hours before arranging. Remove lower florets and top ones will open.

Erica
Heather
Small shrubby foliage in various shades of green and bronze, and clusters of flowers ranging in colour from white to purple.
CARE Cut stem ends and place in deep water.

Eryngium
Sea Holly
Thistle-like spiny flowers with a bluish, metallic sheen. Good dried for winter decoration indoors.
CARE Place in deep water.

Eucalyptus
Eucalyptus
Foliage plants, silver-blue in colour. Also useful in dried-flower arrangements.
CARE Cut the stems and remove lower foliage.

Eucharis
Eucharis Lily
Large fragrant flowers, creamy-white in colour, carried in clusters of four to six on medium-tall stems.
CARE Place in water with cut-flower feed. Keep away from drafts. Mist to add humidity.

Euonymus
Euonymus
Deciduous varieties used for autumn foliage and bright-red fruits. Evergreens have variegated gold, silver or pink tightly packed leaves.
CARE Cut and slit stem ends.

Euphorbia fulgens
Scarlet Plume
Clusters of small flowers surrounded by scarlet bracts.
CARE Plunge stem ends in boiling water. Sap may irritate skin. Remove lower foliage.

Euphorbia marginata
Snow-on-the-mountain
Oblong leaves, upper ones with white margins. Flowers held in umbels which have surrounding white bracts.
CARE Plunge stem ends in boiling water. Sap may irritate skin.

Euphorbia myrsinites
Spurge
Long-lasting, bright yellow-green blooms, attractive in cut-flower arrangements. Small, pointed grayish leaves.
CARE Plunge stem ends in boiling water for 5 seconds. Sap may irritate skin.

Euphorbid pulcherrima
Poinsettia
Small, greenish-red flowers are surrounded by bracts in bright red, pink, yellow or white.
CARE Plunge stem ends in boiling water. Sap may irritate skin.

Eustoma
Lisianthus
White or blue bell-shaped flowers – either individual blooms or in panicles.
CARE Cut stem ends.

F

Fagus
Beech
Attractive foliage for flower arrangements, coloured green, gold or purple.
CARE Cut and slit stem ends.

Fatsia
Fatsia
Foliage plant with large, long-lasting, and deeply cut leaves.
CARE Cut stem ends.

Foeniculum
Fennel
Foliage plant with feathery, finely cut leaves in either green or bronze.
CARE Cut stem ends

Forsythia
Forsythia
Graceful architectural woody stems lined with small, yellow star-shaped flowers.
CARE Cut woody stem ends and place in deep water.

Freesia
Freesia
Highly fragrant sprays of long-lasting, trumpet-shaped flowers in a wide array of colours, including white, cream, mauve or pink.
CARE Place in deep water with cut-flower feed.

Fritillaria imperialis
Crown Imperial
Tall straight stems stopped with a rosette of bell-shaped orange or yellow flowers.
CARE Place in deep water for a few hours before arranging. Change water frequently.

Fritillaria meleagris
Snake's Head Fritillary
Attractive, nodding bell-shaped flowers on slim stems – either plain or chequered white or purple.
CARE Place in deep water for a few hours before arranging.

G

Gaillardia
Gaillardia
Long-stemmed, disc-shaped flowers in red, yellow, purple or orange, often having contrasting edges.
CARE Place in deep water for a few hours before arranging.

Galanthus
Snowdrop
Long-lasting, bell-shaped white flowers with a drooping habit. Large outer petals and smaller inner ones marked with green. Slender, basal leaves.
CARE Cut stem ends and place in cool shallow water.

Galax
Galax
Attractive foliage plant with shiny leathery leaves which are basically heart-shaped and tufted. Beautiful bronze colour in autumn and long-lasting when cut.
CARE Preserve before arranging by wrapping in damp paper.

Gardenia
Gardenia
Highly scented yellow or white flowers, available in single or double varieties. These flowers are easily bruised or otherwise damaged and must be handled with great care when being transported and arranged.
CARE Mist and keep cool, but keep away from drafts.

Garrya
Garrya
Pendulous silver-gray catkins and glossy-green leaves.
CARE Cut woody stem ends and place in deep water for a few hours before arranging.

Gaylussacia
Huckleberry
Oblong or egg-shaped shiny leves. Small, bell-shaped flowers in white, pink or red, followed by black fruits.
CARE Preserve before arranging by wrapping in damp paper.

Genista
Broom
Soft, arching branches of brilliantly golden, small and fragrant pea-like flowers. Only sparse foilage
CARE Cut or slit stem ends and plunge in boiling water.

Gentiana
Gentian
Trumpet-shaped, intense-blue flowers, most often short-stemmed. Attractive flower colour in arrangements.
CARE Place in water in a bright warm position, away from drafts.

Gerbera
Gerbera
Long-lasting, daisy-shaped flowers in yellow, orange, purple, cream or red.
CARE Cut stem end and protect flower head if limp. Arrange when firm.

Geum
Geum
Nodding heads of either orange, yellow, white or red flowers.
CARE Plunge stem ends in boiling water.

Gladiolus
Gladiolus
Tall, long-lasting stems of brightly coloured flowers.
CARE Cut stems under water, and cut again every few days.

Gloriosa
Glory Lily
Stems of red or yellow lily-like flowers with attractive wavy margins.
CARE Cut stem ends at an angle and place in deep water.

Godetia
Godetia
Delicate poppy-like flowers, in single or double types, in either plain or multi-coloured white, pink, orange, salmon or crimson.
CARE Cut stem ends and place in deep water. Lukewarm water and light encourages buds to open.

Gomphrena
Gomphrena
Tightly packed petals making up large flower heads in purple, red, white or yellow.
CARE Place in deep water before arranging.

Grevillea
Grevillea
Foliage plant with feathery leaves and small, tubular, cream-coloured flowers.
CARE Cut stem ends and place in deep water before arranging.

Gypsophila
Gypsophila
Dainty sprays of tiny white or pink flowers.
CARE Cut stem ends regularly and put in deep water.

H

Haemanthus
Blood Lily
Large dense heads of scarlet-coloured flowers on tall stems. Thin oblong leaves carried on separate stems.
CARE Cut stem ends. Place in water with cut-flower feed in warm position.

Hamamelis
Witch Hazel
Fragrant yellow flowers in winter, clustered on bare crooked branches. Four narrow, strap-shaped petals.
CARE Crush woody stem ends and place in deep water.

Hebe
Hebe
Freely-borne flower clusters in mauve, pink or white. Also useful as foliage plant.
CARE Cut stem ends.

Hedera
Ivy
Lobe-shaped leaves, solid green or variegated, in a wide array of sizes.
CARE Cut stem ends and place in deep water.

Helianthus
Sunflower
Flower heads, some of monumental size, with golden-yellow petals radiating from a large, dark centre.
CARE Cut stem ends.

Helichrysum
Straw Flower
Colourful, daisy-shaped bracts in red, orange, gold, pink, yellow or white. (What appear as petals are actually bracts.) Useful in dried-flower arrangements. Narrow, rough leaves.
CARE Remove lower leaves.

Heliconia
Heliconia
Large, long-lasting leaves, some with contrasting veining in either yellow or red. Many also have colourful bracts.
CARE Cut stems straight across.

Heliotrope
Heliotrope
Fragrant vanilla-scented heads of purple, white or lavender-coloured flowers.
CARE Seal stem ends with a naked flame.

Helipterum
Everlasting Daisy
Rose-pink, mauve or white daisy-like flowers.
CARE Place in deep water for a few hours before arranging.

Helleborus
Hellebore
Long-lasting, cup-shaped white, green or purple flowers. Some are spotted.
CARE Cut stem ends and place in warm water.

Hemerocallis
Day Lily
Multi-flowered, leafless stems of trumpet-shaped blooms in either yellow, orange or red.
CARE Place in deep water before arranging.

Heracleum
Hogweed
Large, flat-topped clusters of small white or pinkish flowers. Some of the varieties may be as tall as 8ft (2.5 m).
CARE Very irritating to skin. Wash stems under running water.

Heuchera
Heuchera
Delicate stems of bell-shaped flowers in red, coral or pink.
CARE Place in deep water.

Hibiscus
Hibiscus
Large, open trumpets in red, orange, yellow, pink, white or blue, sometimes with a contrasting basal blotching.
CARE Cut stem ends and plunge in boiling water.

Hippeastrum
Amaryllis
Trumpet-shaped flowers in red, apricot, white or pink. Some striped or edged with contrasting colour.
CARE Insert thin cane into hollow stem to support flower head. Hollow stems may split so put adhesive tape on stem end.

Hosta
Hosta
Leaves in shades of green to blue, with violet, mauve or white spikes of flowers.
CARE Soak leaves in water for a few hours before arranging.

Humulus
Hop
Heavily lobed and serrated leaves. Small, greenish flower-like bracts, which later develop into hops.
CARE Cut and slit stem ends and place in deep water.

Hyacinthus
Hyacinth
Heavy spikes of waxy, bell-shaped fragrant flowers in white, blues, pinks, purples, creams and reds.
CARE Cut stem ends and wipe off any excess sap.

Hydrangea
Hydrangea
Large, long-lasting, cut flowers appearing in either pink, blue or white. Lace-cap and mop-head types available.
CARE Soak heads in cool water for a few hours.

Hypericum
Hypericum
Open cup-shaped flowers, usually yellow in colour.
CARE Cut stem ends and place in deep water.

I

Ilex
Holly
Glossy-green or variegated spiny leaves with clusters of yellow, red or black berries.
CARE Cut stem ends and place in deep water.

Iris
Iris
Three upright and three hanging petals make up the heads of these long-stemmed flowers. They appear in a rainbow of different colours.
CARE Cut off white parts of stems and remove individual flower heads as they die.

Ixia
African Corn Lily
Graceful grassy stems support star-shaped flowers often containing an eye of contrasting colour.
CARE Cut the stem ends and place in cool, deep water.

J

Jasminum
Jasmine
Winter-flowering varieties have long-lasting, yellow, star-shaped flowers on slim arched stems. Summer-flowering varieties have clusters of fragrant, white flowers on twisting stems.
CARE Cut stem ends and place in deep water.

K

Kalanchoe
Kalanchoe
Masses of star-shaped flowers in bright red or yellow.
CARE Place in deep water.

Kalmia
Calico Bush
Clusters of pinky-rose, lantern-shaped flowers with highlights. Shiny-green, oval-shaped leaves.
CARE Cut woody stem ends.

Kerria
Kerria
Golden-yellow single or double flowers with toothed leaves on arching stems.
CARE Cut stem ends.

Kniphofia
Red Hot Poker
Tall thick stems, topped with spikes of either yellow, orange or red flowers.
CARE Place in deep water after cutting.

L

Laburnum
Laburnum
Branches of pendulous racemes of small yellow pea-shaped flowers
CARE Slit stem ends and plunge in boiling water.

Lachenalia
Cape Cowslip
Hanging tubular bells of red, yellow or green flowers.
CARE Place in deep water.

Lathyrus
Sweet Pea
Fragrant, pea-shaped flowers on slender stems. Very varied colours available.
CARE Cut stem ends and place in cool position. Too many stems together cause flowers to die.

Laurus
Bay Laurel
Stems of glossy, oval-shaped leaves with wavy margins.
CARE Submerge in water for a few hours before arranging.

Lavandula
Lavender
Densely growing long stems of highly fragrant mauve flowers, with delicate silver-gray foliage.
CARE Place in deep water.

Lavatera
Mallow
Tall, trumpet-shaped flowers in pink or white. Annual varieties have better colours.
CARE Plunge stem ends in boiling water. Stand in water for several hours.

Leptospermum
Tea Tree
Branches of massed open cup-shaped flowers in white, pink and red. Also has small, leathery leaves. Useful in dried-flower arrangements.
CARE Cut stem ends and place in deep water before arranging.

Leucadendron
Silverbush
Silky, down-covered leaves and heavy fruiting heads of cone-like flowers.
CARE Cut and slit stem ends.

Leucospermum
Leucospermum
Red or yellow flowers, either solitary or in bract-like clusters, contrasting with soft-gray leathery leaves.
CARE Cut stems at an angle.

Liatris
Gay Feathers
Small spikes of densely packed purple flowers.
CARE Cut stem ends and place in deep water for a few hours before arranging.

Ligustrum
Privet
Foliage plant with narrow, oval-shaped green or yellow leaves. White flowers are then followed by black berries.
CARE Cut woody stem ends.

Lilium
Lily
Magnificent trumpet-shaped flowers that appear in a wide array of colours, except blue.
CARE Cut stem ends, place in water overnight and use cut-flower feed. Remove lower foliage.

Limonium
Limonium
Long-lasting cut flowers in many colours, including red or blue. Also good to use in dried-flower arrangements.
CARE Place in deep water for a few hours before arranging.

Lobelia erinus
Lobelia
Small delicate flowers, either white, sky-blue or deep blue. Short-lived when cut.
CARE Place in deep water for a few hours before arranging.

Lobelia fulgens
Cardinal Flower
Lance-shaped, tooth-edged leaves which have tall spikes of bright-crimson flowers.
CARE Place in deep water for a few hours before arranging.

Lonicera
Honeysuckle
Clusters of fragrant, tube-like flowers in white, yellow or scarlet growing on flexible vines.
CARE Cut stem ends and place in deep water before arranging.

Lunaria
Honesty
Stems of purple flowers in summer with flat, disc-like seedheads in autumn. Useful in dried-flower arrangements.
CARE Place in hot water for a few hours before arranging.

Lupinus
Lupin
Tall dense spikes of brightly coloured, pea-shaped flower clusters.
CARE Fill stems with water; plug with cotton wool or put immediately in water to avoid an air lock.

Lysimachia
Loosestrife
Erect stems of yellow flowers framed by pointed oval-shaped leaves.
CARE Place in deep water.

M

Mahonia
Mahonia
Sprays of scented yellow
flowers, followed by black
fruits. Leaves are holly-like
and barbed.
*CARE Cut stem ends and
place in warm water.*

Malus
Crab Apple
Clusters of white or pink
flowers followed by attractive
fruits ranging from deep red
to yellow.
CARE Cut woody stem ends.

Matricaria
Matricaria
Disc-shaped flowers, single
or double forms, and either
white or yellow in colour.
*CARE Remove lower leaves
and place in cool position.*

Matthiola
Stock
Single or double rosette-
shaped flowers in a wide
array of colours, including
buff, lilac and brilliant red,
*CARE Remove lower leaves
and crush stem ends. Change
the water frequently.*

Mentha
Mint
This large family of aromatic
plants is generally useful for
its foliage, ranging from the
bright-green leaves of
spearmint to the white-
edged leaves of applemint.
CARE Place in deep water.

Moluccella
Moluccella
Stems of small flowers, each
surrounded by a cup-shaped,
green-coloured calyx which
is popular for use in flower
arrangements.
*CARE Remove lower leaves
and cut stem ends frequently.*

Monarda
Bergamot
Spiky terminal clusters
of long-lasting fragrant
flowers, in either scarlet,
lilac, pink or white
CARE Place in deep water.

Musa
Banana Leaf
Foliage plants with oblong-
shaped leaves up to 20 ft
(6 m) long. Dwarf varieties
have leaves that are 3 – 6 ft
(1 – 2 m) long.
CARE Spray leaves regularly.

Muscari
Grape Hyacinth
Long-lasting, arrow-shaped
clusters of bluebell-shaped
flowers on short stems. Long,
narrow, dark-green leaves.
*CARE Place in deep water for
a few hours before arranging.*

Myosotis
Forget-me-not
Heads of small powder-blue
flowers with attractively
contrasting yellow eyes.
*CARE Cut stem ends and place
in deep water before arranging.*

Myrtus
Myrtle
Abundant, creamy-white
flowers and densely growing
aromatic bright-green leaves.
CARE Cut woody stem ends.

N

Narcissus
Daffodil
Elegant, trumpet-shaped
flowers, usually yellow
or white. Six petals with
a central trumpet.
*CARE Leave in water overnight
to remove excess sap before
arranging with other flowers.*

Neillia
Neillia
Racemes of pink or white
tubular-shaped flowers.
*CARE Cut stem ends and place
in deep water for a few hours
before arranging.*

Nelumbo
Lotus
Fragrant flowers like water
lilies in pink, rose or white.
Large, shield-like leaves on
long stems.
*CARE If in flower, place in very
deep waer. If with seed heads, cut
stems straight across.*

Nepeta
Catmint
Delicate, lavender-coloured
flowers on long stems, with
small silvery leaves.
*CARE Place in warm water for
a few hours before arranging.*

Nerine
Guernsey Lily
Clusters of lily-like, deep-
pink to near-white flowers
with long stems.
*CARE Cut stem ends and place
in warm water before arranging.*

Nerium
Oleander
Showy, funnel-shaped flowers,
sometimes fragrant, in white,
pink, red or yellow.
*CARE Slit stem ends and plunge
in boiling water.*

Nicotiana
Tobacco Plant
Tall stems of fragrant tubular
flowers, either white, green,
pink or crimson.
*CARE Remove lower leaves and
place in warm water for a few
hours before arranging.*

Nigella
Love-in-a-mist
Best-known in baby blue but
also appears in pink, purple,
rose and white flowers.
*CARE Place in deep water for a
few hours before arranging.*

O

Ocimum
Basil
Aromatic herb-garden plant
with clusters of small white
or purplish flowers.
CARE Cut stems at an angle.

Oenothera
Evening Primrose
Tall spikes of fragrant
yellow flowers that turn
reddich as they age. Buds
open successively, giving
an extended display.
*CARE Plunge stem ends
in boiling water.*

Oncidium
Dancing Lady Orchid
Long arching or erect stems
of small flowers, commonly
greenish-yellow or rose-lilac,
often with blotched lips.
*CARE Cut stem ends at an
angle; cut again every few days.*

Onopordum
Scotch Thistle
Tall plants with toothed or
lobed woolly leaves; head of
spiny purple or white flowers.
*CARE Plunge stem ends in
boiling water.*

Origanum
Marjoram
Low, mould-growing
aromatic plants with small
green leaves and mauve,
pink or white flowers.
CARE Cut stem ends.

Ornithogalum
Star of Bethlehem
Long-lasting, greenish-white
star-shaped flowers also
known as Chincherinchee.
*CARE Cut stem ends. Remove
individual flowers as they die.*

Osteospermum
Osteospermum
Heads of daisy-like
flowers in white, blue, pink
or purple. Flowers often have
contrasting centre colours.
CARE Cut stems straight across.

P

Paeonia
Peony
Large single or double
blooms in white, pink, yellow
or crimson – some having a
contrasting centre.
*CARE Cut stem ends and stand
in deep water before arranging.*

Papaver
Poppy
Delicate cup-shaped flowers
with papery petals in a wide
array of colours. Not long-
lived as cut flowers.
*CARE Seal stem ends with
a naked flame.*

Paphiopedilum
Lady's Slipper Orchid
Long-lasting, single-flowered
stems, varying greatly in size,
shape and colour.
*CARE Cut stem ends at an
angle; cut again every few days.*

Pelargonium
Geranium
Red, coral, pink or white
flowers often beautifully
marked in contrasting
colours. Foliage sometimes
scented or zonally marked.
*CARE Place in deep water for
a few hours before arranging.*

Petroselinum
Parsley
Medium-tall foliage plant with
bright-green, curling leaves.
Not long-lasting if placed
in arrangements.
CARE No special requirements.

Phalaenopsis
Moth Orchid
Usually single stems with up
to 30 white or pale pink
flowers, with lips and throats
often in contrasting colours.
*CARE Cut stem ends at an
angle; cut again every few days.*

Philadelphus
Mock Orange
Freely borne clusters of
sweetly scented white flowers
with yellow stamens.
*CARE Cut woody stem ends
and place in warm water for a
few hours before arranging.*

Phlomis
Jerusalem Sage
Whorls of yellow flowers;
woolly light-green leaves.
*CARE Cut stem ends and place
in deep water.*

Phlox
Phlox
Large clusters of small round
flowers in a wide array of
colours. Often fragrant.
*CARE Cut stem ends and stand
in deep water.*

Phoenix
Palm Leaf
Graceful foliage plant
with narrow leathery leaflets
making up tall, curving hands.
CARE Spray leaves regularly.

Phormium
New Zealand Flax
Stately foliage plant with
green sword-like leaves, with
yellow, bronze, purple or
cream variegations.
*CARE Cut the stem ends
underwater.*

Physalis
Chinese Lantern
Lantern-shaped pods in bright
orange. Also useful in dried-
flower arrangements.
*CARE If fresh, place in deep
water before arranging.*

Physostegia
Obedient Plant
Spikes of tubular-shaped
white, pink or purple flowers
on tall stems. Leaves are
toothed and lance-like.
CARE: Cut stem ends.

Picea
Spruce
Whirls of needle-like leaf
clusters. Some species
have attractive cones.
*CARE Cut woody stem ends
and place in deep water.*

Pinus
Pine
Radiating clusters of
needle-like leaves, ranging
from light green to dusty blue
in colour. Cones are also an
attractive feature of this plant.
*CARE Cut woody stem ends
and place in deep water.*

Pittosporum
Pittosporum
Green-leaved foliage plant,
lustrous and long-lasting.
Some varieties are variegated.
CARE Cut woody stem ends.

Platycodon
Balloon Flower
Balloon-like buds opening
to long-lasting, bell-shaped
flowers in blue or white.
*CARE Plunge stem ends
in boiling water.*

Polianthes
Tuberose
Stems of sweetly scented,
trumpet-shaped white flowers
that have grass-like leaves.
*CARE Place in deep water for
a few hours before arranging.*

Polygonatum
Solomon's Seal
Waxy-looking, greenish-white
flowers which hang from
gracefully arching stems.
*CARE Place in warm water for
a few hours before arranging.*

Primula auricula
Auricula
Pendulous, bell-shaped flower
clusters of various colours.
Flowers have a distinctive
white centre and yellow eye.
*CARE Cut stem ends and place
in deep water.*

Primula polyantha
Polyanthus
Dense clusters of crimson,
pink, blue, white or yellow
primrose-like flowers.
*CARE Cut stem ends and
place in deep water.*

Primula veris
Cowslip
Bright-yellow umbels of small,
and often fragrant, flowers.
Leaves oval and mid-green.
*CARE Cut stem ends and put
in deep water for a few hours
before arranging.*

Primula vulgaris
Primrose
Single-flower stems forming
loosely rounded heads of
creamy-yellow blooms with
bright yellow eyes.
*CARE Cut stem ends and put
in deep water for a few hours
before arranging.*

Protea
Protea
Extravagantly large, long-
lasting flowers which appear
many colours.
*CARE Cut stem ends and place
in deep water. Cut frequently.*

Prunus
Flowering Cherry
Elegant architectural branches
with sprays of white, pink or
red spring flowers.
CARE Cut woody stem ends.

Pteris
Ribbon Brake Fern
Foliage plant with wavy-
edged, ribbon-like leaves.
Creamy-white centres
and green margins.
*CARE Seal stem ends with
a naked flame.*

Pyracantha
Firethorn
Thorny branches of bright-
yellow, orange or red berries
and small glossy leaves.
CARE Cut woody stem ends.

Pyrethrum
Pyrethrum
Hairy, fern-like leaves and
daisy-shaped flowers in white,
salmon, pink or scarlet.
*CARE Cut stem ends and
place in deep water.*

R

Ranunculus
Buttercup
Long-lasting, cup-shaped
single or double blooms in
yellow, white or red.
*CARE Place in deep water for a
few hours before arranging.*

Reseda
Mignonette
Heads of fragrant yellowish-
white, greenish-white or
red flowers.
*CARE Plunge stem ends
in boiling water.*

Rheum
Rhubarb
Foliage plant with broad,
flat, heart-shaped leaves and
prominent veining. Leaves
are poisonous.
*CARE Submerge leaves briefly
in cool water.*

Rhododendron
Rhododendron
Large family of plants,
typically with shiny leathery
foliage and clusters of large
funnel-shaped flowers.
*CARE Cut woody stem ends
and plunge in boiling water.*

Ribes
Flowering Currant
Stems of pink or white
pendulous flower clusters
with lobed leaves.
*CARE Cut woody stem ends
and place in deep water.*

Rosa
Rose
Large array of colours, sizes
and shapes. Single and multi-
stemmed varieties. Flowers
are usually fragrant.
*CARE Cut stem ends and
place in deep water.*

Rosmarinus
Rosemary
Spiny, aromatic leaves
along with small mauve-
white flowers.
*CARE Cut stem ends and
place in deep water. Remove
lower foliage.*

Rubus
Bramble
Prickly stems of attractive
foliage and white, pink or
purple flowers, similar in
shape to the dog rose. These
are followed by black or red
fruits in the autumn.
*CARE Cut and slit stem ends
and place in deep water for a few
hours before arranging.*

Rudbeckia
Cone Flower
Daisy-like flowers,
ranging from deep yellow
to orange in colour, with a
contrasting dark eye.
*CARE Cut stem ends
and place in water.*

Rumex
Dock
The fat, rosy-red seed
pods are the plant's chief
feature, making a very
decorative addition to
a flower arrangement.
*CARE Cut the stems
at an angle.*

Ruscus
Butcher's Broom
Deep-green leaves with
tiny green and purple
flowers, also scarlet or
yellow berries.
*CARE Cut stem ends and
place in deep water for a
few hours before arranging.*

Ruta
Rue
Aromatic, pungent herb
with feathery, bluish
leaves and tiny yellow
flowers which are rather
like buttercups.
*CARE Cut stem ends
and place in deep water.*

S

Salix
Willow
A large species of
plants, many displaying
an attractive bark and
catkins as well as leaves.
*CARE Cut stem ends
and place in deep water.*

Salpiglossis
Salpiglossis
Wide-throated, funnel-
shaped flowers in scarlet,
yellow, crimson, mauve
or cream, showing a
contrasting veining.
CARE Place in deep water.

Sandersonia
Sandersonia
Bright-yellow flowers on
drooping graceful stems,
with lance-shaped leaves.
*CARE Cut the stems
at an angle.*

Sanservieria
Mother-in-law's Tongue
Tall fleshy leaves,
erect and green, often
variegated and mottled.
Pale greenish-white
blooms which are
long-lasting when cut.
*CARE Cut the stems
at an angle.*

Santolina
Lavender Cotton
Divided foilage which is
a silvery-gray colour
along with only insignificant,
ball-shaped yellow flowers
rather like pompoms.
*CARE Cut stem ends
and place in deep water
for a few hours before arranging.*

Saponaria
Soapwort
Small pink, white or
purple star-like flowers.
Leaves are very flat and
broad. Flowers last longer
if they are arranged as a
single-species display.
CARE Place in cool position.

Sarracenia
Pitcher Plant
Exotic insectivorous
plants with leaves that are
shaped like deep funnels
or pitchers, in which they
trap their prey.
CARE Place in very deep water.

Scabiosa
Scabious
Open, ruffled flowers in
varied colours of blue,
mauve, crimson or white.
*CARE Cut stem ends and place
in deep water for a few hours.*

Scilla non-scripta
Bluebell
Stems of pendulous
bell-shaped flowers in blue,
pink or white. Short-lived
as cut flowers.
CARE Place in deep water.

Scilla sibirica
Squill
Brilliant-blue, drooping
flower heads held on
delicate stems. Short-
lived as cut flowers.
CARE Place in deep water.

Sedum
Sedum
Densely packed tiny flowers
forming flat heads of pink,
blue or mauve. Grayish-
green foliage.
*CARE Cut the stem ends at
angle and put in deep water
before arranging.*

Seneico
Cineraria
Attractively felted silver-
gray foliage and clusters
of yellow daisy-like flowers.
*CARE Cut stem ends and
place in warm water for a
few hours before arranging.*

Skimmia
Skimmia
Clusters of fragrant
star-shaped flowers,
followed by bright-red
fruits in winter.
*CARE Cut stem ends an
place in warm water for a
few hours before arranging.*

Solidago
Golden Rod
Tall feathery plumes of
tiny yellow flowers with
rough foliage. Small
lance-shaped green leaves.
*CARE Place in deep
water for a few hours
before arranging.*

Sorbus
White Beam
Branches with large
clusters of white flowers
and large silver-green leaves.
*CARE Cut stem ends and place
in deep water for a few hours
before arranging.*

Sparaxis
Wandflower
Short spikes of star-shaped
flowers, often with a dark
eye, in lilac, pink, crimson,
yellow, orange or cream.
*CARE Cut stem ends and place
in deep water before arranging.*

Spiraea
Spirea
Slender branches which
have dense clusters of
tiny white flowers.
CARE Cut woody stem ends.

Stachys
Lamb's Ears
Foliage plant with stems
of small, gray downy leaves.
Insignificant purple or pink
flowers in summer.
*CARE Remove the foilage
underwater.*

Stephanotis
Waxflower
Dark-green shiny foliage
with star-shaped, waxy-
white flowers in stark
contrast. These fragrant
flowers bruise easily and
are used mainly in short-
lived arrangements, such as
bridal headdresses.
*CARE Cut stem ends and
place in water.*

Strelitzia
Bird of Paradise
Brightly coloured orange
and blue, bird-shaped flowers
with an orange crest.
*CARE Cut stem ends at an
angle and place in deep water.*

Symphoricarpos
Snowberry
Used mainly for their pink
or white berries that appear
on long stems.
*CARE Remove excess leaves.
Scrape and slit stem ends.*

Syringa
Lilac
Large trusses of fragrant
flowers in varying shades
of purple through to white.
*CARE Cut stem ends and place
in water with cut-flower feed.*

T

Tanacetum
Tansy
Dense clusters of small,
button-like flowers with a
fern-like fragrant foliage.
*CARE Remove lower leaves
and cut stem ends.*

Tellima
Tellima
Useful foliage plant with
stems of heart-shaped
leaves and small green or
pink bell-shaped flowers.
*CARE Plunge stem ends in
boiling water.*

Telopea
Waratah
Striking red globular
flower heads with red
bracts. Long, leathery
tooth-edged leaves.
CARE Cut woody stem ends.

Thymus
Thyme
Aromatic, low-growing
herb with small purple,
pink or crimson flowers.
*CARE Place in deep water for
a few hours before arranging.*

Tiarella
Tiarella
Heart-shaped, mottled
foliage and dainty spikes
of cream or pink flowers.
*CARE Submerge leaves
completely in cool water for a
few hours before arranging.*

Tilia
Lime
Small, fragrant yellow-green
cluster flowers. Remove or
reduce excess foliage.
*CARE Crush stem ends and
place in deep water for a few
hours before arranging.*

Trachelium
Trachelium
Small white, purple or blue
long-lasting flowers in dense
terminal heads. Buy only
when a few flowers are open.
CARE Cut stem ends.

Tricyrtis
Toad Lily
Long-stemmed plants
with spotted bell-shaped,
mauve flowers and
slender pointed leaves.
*CARE Place in deep water for
a few hours before arranging.*

Triticum
Wheat
Tall, grass-like plants with
large seedheads. May be
used fresh or dried.
CARE Cut stems at an angle.

Trollius
Globe Flower
Long-lasting, globe-shaped
flowers in orange or yellow.
*CARE Cut stem ends and
plunge in boiling water.*

Tropaeolum
Nasturtium
Long-lasting flowers with vivid
orange or red trumpets.
Splendid as cut flowers.
CARE Place in deep water.

Tulipa
Tulip
Simple waxy flowers in a
huge range of colours – with
striped and spotted varieties.
*CARE Wash off excess sap
and soil. Cut at an angle.*

Typha
Typha
Dark-brown to black
ornamental pokers with
thin, strap-like leaves.
CARE Place in deep water.

V

Vaccinium
Cowberry
Glossy-green, oval-shaped
leaves, with small bell-shaped
white flowers and red or
black autumn or fall berries.
CARE Cut woody stem ends.

Vallota
Scarborough Lily
Long-lasting stems of large,
funnel-shaped, glowing
orange/scarlet flowers.
CARE Cut stems at an angle.

Verbascum
Verbascum
Tall spikes of trumpet-shaped
flowers, usually yellow. Some
pink forms available. Silver-
gray woolly leaves.
CARE Remove lower foliage.

Verbena
Verbena
Flat, compact clusters
of small purple, red, blue,
cream or white flowers
on short stems.
CARE Place in deep water.

Veronica
Veronica
Tapering spikes of mainly
lilac-blue flowers. Flowers
also pink and white. Leaves
are slender and pointed.
CARE Place in deep water.

Viburnum
Guelder Rose
Pendulous clusters of
red berries beneath
well-lobed, deep-green
leaves. Also has fragrant
white flowers.
*CARE Cut stem ends and use
flower feed for woody stems.*

Vinca
Periwinkle
Long strands of dark-
green, oval-shaped leaves
dotted with pale-blue
flowers. Several mauve
and white forms are
also available.
*CARE Soak strands in
water for several hours.*

Viola odorata
Violet
Sweetly scented velvety
flowers, usually deep
purple but also in pink,
white, biscuit, pale blue
and yellow.
*CARE Submerge flowers in
cool water overnight. Spray
the arrangement frequently.*

Viola tricolor
Pansy
Open-faced, five-petalled
flowers in a wide array
of colours, often with
strongly contrasting
colour patches.
CARE Place in deep water.

Viscum
Mistletoe
Parasitic plant with
jointed woody stems
and long-lasting
white berries.
*CARE Cut the stem
ends at an angle.*

Vitis
Grape Vine
Deeply lobed leaves
with rich autumn colour.
Stems have clinging
tendrils and clusters of
green or black fruits.
*CARE Plunge stem ends
in boiling water.*

W

Watsonia
Watsonia
Funnel-shaped flowers
growing either side of
stems are apricot, red,
pink or orange in colour.
Sword-shaped leaves are
similar in form to the
gladiolus.
*CARE Cut the stems
underwater and then cut
again every few days.*

Weigela
Weigela
Dense clusters of
trumpet-shaped flowers
in either red, pink or
white with a coarse foliage
and arching stems.
CARE Cut woody stem ends.

Wisteria
Wisteria
Pendulous racemes of
pea-like flowers in either
purple, lilac or white.
*CARE Place in deep water
for a few hours before arranging.*

X

Xeranthemum
Immortelle
Disc-dhaped, paper-like
bracts of white, rose or
purple, held on long stems.
*CARE Place in deep water for
a few hours before arranging.*

Z

Zantedeschia
Arum Lily
Funnel-shaped flowers
in either white, pink, green
or yellow, with large
yellow spadix.
*CARE Place in deep warm
water, submerging the leaves.*

Zea
Maize
Tall grass-like plants
with bulbous seed heads,
sheathed in bracts or
husks with a lining of
silk-like threads. Useful
for displaying in dried-
flower arrangements.
*CARE Cut the stem ends
at an angle.*

Zinnia
Zinnia
Large ball- or daisy-
shaped dazzling flowers,
available in either single-
toned, multi-coloured
or striped forms.
*CARE Cut stem ends
above leaf joint and
plant in water.*

Index

LATIN INDEX

GENERAL INDEX

ACKNOWLEDGMENTS

This book took over 18 months to put together and by the end of that period I realized how many good friends and colleagues I have. The project has involved a cast of hundreds and the contribution of family, friends, colleagues, clients and customers – to them I express my sincere gratitude and appreciation. Creating this book has been a labour of love not only on my part but also on the part of the dedicated few around me, to them my most heartfelt thanks.

First, thanks to the constant support and advice of Dennis Edwards of John Austin & Company Ltd. Dennis believed in me when my bank had doubts and he imported and supplied almost all of the wonderful flowers in this book. Quite simply without him the project would not have been possible and I am immensely grateful to him and his team at Stand M5 at New Covent Garden in London.

Thanks also to Jacqui Small whom I first knew as a customer. From her Saturday forays into my shop in Islington she offered me the opportunity to create this book and her practical advice and love of flowers have been inspiring. On the inspirational side a very large thank you is due also to Ashleigh Hopkins who manages my shop and is an immensely talented florist. I am indebted to her for arranging my ideas and contributing her own imaginative designs for this book. She has also kept my business running and put in an enormous amount of unpaid time over the years, so thanks to her for her dedication.

It was a great privilege to work with Kevin Summers, whose contribution to this book is immeasurable and I am enormously grateful for his talent and imagination in creating the photographs. Thanks also to Sara Morris and Cameron Watt for assisting with the photography and for the backgrounds, which are by Tabby Riley.

The team at Mitchell Beazley also worked very hard. A long-suffering Sophie deserves an award for her patience and understanding, without her I would probably never have got the text off to the printers and the pages would still be full of white space! Thanks also to Judith More who quietly encouraged me and was sympathetic to other pressures which sometimes prevented me from sitting down at my word processor and allowed a deadline to slip! Thank you too to Trinity Fry who spent many extra hours making sure that the visual side of the book looked perfect – I think her design work speaks for itself. Trin also helped to present my arrangements for the photographs and the book is a credit to her after careful poring over the transparencies.

Whenever I disappeared into Kevin's studio for a week of photography, the rest of my staff had to work much harder than usual and I am very grateful to them for their support. Thank you also to all Paula Pryke Flowers helpers past and present, and in particular to those who worked on the book: Ashleigh, whom I have already mentioned, Tadhg Ryan who put in many unpaid hours of assistance, Amanda Lovegrove, Nicky Walker, Lizzie Ruse, Ann Pochetty, Val Singer, Caren Galea, Karen Groves, Jean Moore, Leanne Zenonos, Tracy Sedgewick, Nicola Sissons, Dee Kendal, Heidi Hooper, Rebecca Jewell, Hayley Papworth, Heidi Meadows, Leanda Xavain, Elizabeth Price and finally a very special thank you to Gina Jay. For the introductory chapter on the world flower market I am grateful to Marcel Van Eijsden from MHG Flowers and for his patience and assistance as our guide in the Netherlands and for his help in identifying all the wonderful flowers in this book; thanks also to Foppe Meijaer.

Thank you also to Nigel Slater for making the edible Valentine's Day heart and for his time, support and encouragement and for being such a pleasant person to work with. Angela Flanders supplied the candles and the pot pourri for the book and I am grateful to her for all her help. A big thank you is also due to Terry and Jean Chivers who gave me the opportunity to work with flowers and who have taught me so much. Also warm thanks to all my clients and customers who have been so supportive while I have been away working on the book. Last, and by no means least, thank you to my wonderful husband Peter whom I met before I became so passionate about flowers and who has shared the ups and downs of it all. Thank you for your love and support.

The author and publishers would also like to thank: Linda Helm Antiques, Dean Gipson from Deans Antiques, Nicola Phillips at L.A.S.S.C.O., Susan Palmer Antiques, Michael Lewis Antiques, Sir Terence Conran, John Gardener from Arnott and Mason, everyone at Ronald Porter & Sons, Hugh Bradnum at Geest, Martin Ray from John Ray Ltd, Linda and Kees Ros at C. Ros Flowers, Ted Lawrence at Geo Munro, Bridget Bodoano at The Conran Shop, Pushpa Gulhane at Aria, Marsha Solon, Terra-Nigra farm, Verseveld Roses, The Royal Horticultural Society and The Flower Council of Holland.